Englishes in Contact
Anglophone Caribbean Students in an Urban College

WRITTEN LANGUAGE
Marcia Farr, senior editor

Perspectives on Written Argument
 Deborah Berrill (ed.)

From Millwrights to Shipwrights to the Twenty-First Century
 R. John Brockmann

Collaboration and Conflict: A Contextual Exploration of Group Writing and Positive Emphasis
 Geoffrey Cross

Contexts, Intertexts, and Hypertexts
 Scott DeWitt and Kip Strasma (eds.)

Subject to Change: New Composition Instructors' Theory and Practice
 Christine Farris

Assessing the Portfolio: Principles for Practice, Theory, and Research
 Liz Hamp-Lyons and William Condon

Writing on the Plaza: Mediated Literacy Practice Among Scribes and Clients in Mexico City
 Judy Kalman

Literacy: Interdisciplinary Conversations
 Deborah Keller-Cohen (ed.)

Literacy Across Communities
 Beverly Moss (ed.)

Artwork of the Mind: An Interdisciplinary Description of Insight and the Search for it in Student Writing
 Mary Murray

Word Processing and the Non-Native Writer
 Martha C. Pennington

Self-Assessment and Development in Writing: A Collaborative Inquiry
 Jane Bowman Smith and Kathleen Blake Yancey

Twelve Readers Reading: Responding to College Student Writing
 Richard Straub and Ronald Lunsford

Validating Holistic Scoring for Writing Assessment: Theoretical and Empirical Foundations
 Michael Williamson and Brian Huot (eds.)

Englishes in Contact

Anglophone Caribbean Students in an Urban College

Shondel J. Nero
St. John's University

HAMPTON PRESS, INC.
CRESSKILL, NEW JERSEY

OHIO UNIVERSITY LIBRARY

Copyright © 2001 by Hampton Press, Inc.

All rights reserved. No part of this publication may be reproduced, stored in a retrieval system, or transmitted in any form or by any means, electronic, mechanical, photocopying, microfilming, recording, or otherwise, without permission of the publisher.

Printed in the United States of America

Library of Congress Cataloging-in-Publication Data

Nero, Shondel J.
   Englishes in contact : Anglophone Caribbean students in an urban college / Shondel J. Nero.
     p. cm. -- (Writen language)
   Includes bibliographical references and indexes.
   ISBN 1-57273-325-X -- ISBN 1-57273-326-8
    1. English language--Caribbean Area. 2. English language--Rhetoric--Study and teaching--New York (State)--New York. 3. College students--New York (State)--New York--Language. 4. English language--Study and teaching--Caribbean Area. 5. Languages in contact--New York (State)--York. 6. College students--Caribbean Area--Language. 7. Creole dialects, English--Caribbean Area. 8. Languages in contact--Caribbean Area 9. English language--Written English. I. Title. II. Series.

PE3302 .N47 2001
420'.9729--dc21

00-050606

Hampton Press, Inc.
23 Broadway
Cresskill, NJ 07626

Contents

Series Preface		ix
Acknowledgments		xi
1.	INTRODUCTION	1
2.	CREOLES, IDENTITY, AND CARIBBEAN MIGRATION	5
	Caribbean English-Based Creoles	5
	Anglophone Caribbean Migration	8
3.	LANGUAGES, DIALECTS AND EDUCATION	11
	Creoles: Languages or Dialects?	11
	Anglophone Caribbean Students in England	14
	Anglophone Caribbean Students in Canadian Schools	16
	Anglophone Caribbean Students in American Schools	17
	Literacies and Writing in an American Context	20
	Research Perspectives	27

4. THE STUDY — 29
- Setting — 29
- Participants — 31
- Data Collection — 32
- Data Analysis — 34

5. CHARLES BENJAMIN — 41
- Early Language and Schooling Experiences — 42
- Migration and Schooling in New York City — 43
- Writing at LIU — 45
- Discourse Analysis — 46
- Final Reflections — 58

6. MYRNA GEORGE — 61
- Early Language and Schooling Experiences — 62
- Migration and Schooling in New York City — 63
- Writing at LIU — 64
- Discourse Analysis — 64
- Final Reflections — 79

7. NADINE FERGUSON — 81
- Migration and Schooling in New York City — 82
- Writing at LIU — 84
- Discourse Analysis — 84
- Final Reflections — 97

8. OSCAR EVANS — 99
- Early Language and Schooling Experiences — 100
- High School in Jamaica — 101
- Writing at LIU — 103
- Discourse Analysis — 104
- Final Reflections — 114

9. DISCUSSION AND CONCLUSIONS — 117
- Style Shifting — 117
- Speech and Writing — 118
- Discourse Features in the Participants' Writing — 119
- Morphosyntactic Features — 123
- Reflections on Four Semesters in the Writing Program — 125
- Placement — 125
- Broader Issues — 126
- Language Attitudes — 127

A "Resource-Full" Policy	131
Directions for Future Research	136

APPENDIX A   139
    Sample Placement Test Followed by Questions   139

APPENDIX B: CHARLES' WRITING SAMPLE   141
    Conversation Between Roger and His Parents   141

APPENDIX C: MYRNA'S WRITING SAMPLE   145
    Unfair Competition in a Dishonest and Racist Society   145

APPENDIX D: NADINE'S WRITING SAMPLE   149
    Too Close for Comfort   149

APPENDIX E: OSCAR'S WRITING SAMPLE   155
    Oral History Research—Bob Marley   155

Notes	159
References	161
Author Index	167
Subject Index	169

Series Preface

This series examines the characteristics of *writing* in the human world. Volumes in the series present scholarly work on written language in its various contexts. Across time and space, human beings use various forms of written language—or writing systems—to fulfill a range of social, cultural, and personal functions, and this diversity can be studied from a variety of perspectives within both the social sciences and the humanities, including those of linguistics, anthropology, psychology, education, rhetoric, literacy criticism, philosophy, and history. Although writing is not often used apart from oral language, or without aspects of reading, and thus many volumes in this series include other facets of language and communication, writing itself receives primary emphasis.

While the study of writing is absorbing in its own right, it is an increasingly important social issue as well, as demographic movements occur around the world and as language and ethnicity accrue more intensely political meanings. Writing, and literacy more generally, is central to education, and education in turn is central to occupational and social mobility.

Manuscripts that present the results of empirical research, both qualitative and quantitative, or theoretical treatments of relevant issues are encouraged for submission.

Acknowledgments

The last five years have been a journey of fun, frustration, stress, excitement and simply longing to "get there." Such is the story of writing a book. Along the way were friends, family, colleagues, and mentors who never stopped believing that I could do this.

Many thanks to my editor, Marcia Farr, and to her assistant, Daiva Markelis, for their professionalism, patience, and expert guidance throughout the review process. I am indebted to the staff at Hampton Press, especially Barbara Bernstein, for their efficiency in expediting the copyediting and publication process. Special thanks to the anonymous reviewers and copyeditor who helped to refine the manuscript.

I gratefully acknowledge the financial and moral support of my dean and colleagues in the School of Education at St. John's University. A summer research grant awarded by the School of Education allowed me to complete the manuscript in a timely fashion.

Thanks to the challenging and caring faculty at Teachers College, Columbia University, especially Clifford Hill, for being a mentor, reader, editor, and most of all, believing in my potential. Special thanks to JoAnne Kleifgen, Frank Horowitz and Lambros Comitas, for their careful reading, constructive criticism and constant support during the early stages of the manuscript. I owe much to Lambros Comitas whose course prompted me to "revisit" the Caribbean.

My deepest appreciation to the four students who participated in this study—Charles, Myrna, Nadine and Oscar—who so graciously gave of their time to share their lives and work with me. I owe them an enormous debt. Many thanks to the English Department at Long Island University, Brooklyn Campus, where this study took place.

Thanks to my linguistics circle at Teachers College—Cynthia McCollie-Lewis, Halima Touré, Jon Yasin, and Charles Coleman—for their moral support and helpful suggestions.

Many thanks to my friends and their families who have listened, supported and wished me only the very best throughout this process—Sonia Bacchus, Jennifer Joe, Brynmor Bowen, Michelle Balée and Xiao-Ming Li.

My heartfelt gratitude to Mom and Dad for their love and support and for always believing in me. Thanks to my brothers and sisters—Trevor, Cherryl, Kwesi, and Dara—and their families who, though across the ocean, have always been there in spirit.

Finally, to my husband and greatest inspiration, Louis Parascandola: Thank you for being there every step of the way—for reading, editing, listening, caring, pushing, but never crowding. Your love and support and, of course, our endless conversations, have sustained me through a worthwhile journey. This one's for you.

1

Introduction

In an autobiographical essay completed in his basic writing class, Charles Benjamin,[1] a native of Guyana, described his romantic relationship with a young woman, which eventually led to the young woman's pregnancy: "So I started talking to a young lady and she got pregnant." Charles' writing instructor responded to this statement with the comment, "big jump," suggesting there was a logical gap between Charles' merely talking to the young woman and her becoming pregnant. The implication here is that a process of acquaintance is normally expected to take place over time before two people bear a child; hence, the instructor expected Charles to elaborate on that presumed acquaintance in transitional sentences. The instructor was obviously unaware that Charles' use of the word "talking" in this context carried the Guyanese Creole English meaning of "getting to know, dating and possibly becoming sexually involved with." With this semantic load in mind, Charles felt that his choice of the word "talking" was perfectly logical, and so he found the instructor's comment puzzling. The instructor, on the other hand, read the word "talking" with the standard English prototypical meaning, that is, "to engage in conversation" and so, quite innocently, missed Charles' intended meaning. Ironically, the very clarification implicitly requested by the instructor's comment had already been (mis)communicated.

The scenario above can recur in various forms in many American college writing classrooms unless writing instructors are appropriately trained to respond to the growing linguistic diversity in our classrooms, especially the increasing number of speakers of "other Englishes" fostered by a significant rise in immigration from the Caribbean region. Charles is one of thousands of immigrants from the officially English-speaking Caribbean (hereafter called the anglophone Caribbean)[2] who have migrated to the United States, especially to New York City, within the last two decades. With this new influx, public schools and colleges are being challenged to educate immigrant students whose native languages might be classified as "other Englishes" or, more precisely, "Caribbean Creole Englishes"—creolized varieties of English that seem markedly different from what school authorities have traditionally defined as English. In strictly linguistic terms, the presence of Caribbean Creole Englishes in our classrooms constitutes merely a question of language learning and teaching. But in a broader context, the ethnolinguistic transformation of American schools invites much needed debate and research on the larger, more complex issues of changing immigration patterns, ethnic and linguistic diversity, language attitudes, and educational responses to linguistic diversity.

It is within this framework that this study was undertaken. The overall goals of the study were: (a) to analyze the language and educational experiences of anglophone Caribbean students; (b) to examine policy, programs and pedagogy that address linguistic diversity with particular attention to Caribbean immigrant students; (c) to provide guidelines for practitioners for teaching standard academic English to Caribbean Creole English-speaking students based on case studies of such students.

Studies of Caribbean Creole English speakers are by no means novel. However, a review of the literature revealed that most of the research in regard to the language and pedagogy of anglophone Caribbean students in North America has been done at the elementary and high school levels (Anderson & Grant, 1987; Coelho, 1991; Narvaez & Garcia, 1992; Pratt-Johnson, 1993; Solomon, 1992; Winer, 1993). Studies have also been done on the writing of college students who are speakers of nonstandard English (Holm, 1985) or African American Vernacular English speakers (Ball, 1992; Coleman, 1995). However, there has been no in-depth study, to my knowledge, on the language and pedagogy of anglophone Caribbean students at the college level. Anglophone Caribbean college students who do not demonstrate the requisite proficiency in standard written English to be placed into a freshman composition class are categorized along with other nonstandard English speakers as *basic writers* (Shaughnessy, 1977) and are typically studied under the same rubric. This study seeks to bridge the gap in the research by investigating the spoken and written language of anglophone Caribbean college students and the educational responses to their language in terms of placement, assessment, reading and writing instruction.

I begin with the premise that language use is socially determined. Therefore, any analysis of a student's language performance in school must include a broader examination of the historical and sociocultural contexts within which the student's language and literacy practices have developed. Anglophone Caribbean students, like many other formerly colonized peoples, find themselves in a unique linguistic situation where they are educated in a language they do not habitually speak (LePage & Tabouret-Keller, 1985). The Creole Englishes spoken by the vast majority of Anglophone Caribbean natives and which emerged from a historical language contact situation have developed within a primarily oral tradition. Until recently, they have had no standardized orthography (Allsopp's [1996] *Dictionary of Caribbean English Usage* has been the most comprehensive project to date to redress this), neither have they been given official recognition as languages in their own right. Most importantly, Creole Englishes are not validated in school or formal domains. When the Creole English speaker comes to school, his/her language is usually judged against standard written academic English with which s/he may be less familiar.

Because English is the official language in the anglophone Caribbean, natives of the region perceive their mother tongue as standard English regardless of their actual level of proficiency in it. This perception is reinforced by the fact that there is a high degree of mutual intelligibility between predominantly Creole English speakers and those who are more proficient in standard English. Cheshire (1991) observes that as English has become nativized in various parts of the world through colonization and global movement, it now includes "typologically distinct varieties as pidgins and creoles, 'new' Englishes and a range of differing standard and nonstandard varieties that are spoken on a regular basis" (p. 1). She contends that "mother tongue" is "not necessarily a useful or meaningful concept" (p. 2) in many parts of the developing world, where "population movement, language loss, language shift, and language attitudes may all affect the language that speakers consider to be their first language" (p. 2). Thus, the distinction between native and nonnative speaker of English in such contexts is becoming increasingly blurred.

The participants in this study can be situated in the "blurry" linguistic area between native and nonnative speakers of English. Though they all considered themselves native speakers of English, their proficiency in spoken English was not necessarily paralleled by competence in the written form, at least not the kind privileged in school. As will be seen from this study, their linguistic performance in school resulted from a combination of factors that ranged from the historical and social to the idiosyncratic.

To come to a better understanding of these Anglophone Caribbean students in North American classrooms, I begin Chapter 2 by offering a sociohistorical background on the genesis and development of Creole Englishes in Caribbean societies. In addition, I examine the linguistic identities, social hierarchies, and educational practices that have emerged in these societies. As part of the background information, I also discuss the factors that have influenced Caribbean migration to North America and the changing profile of anglophone Caribbean immigrants.

Chapter 3 examines the complicated question of whether Creoles should be considered dialects of English or autonomous languages. The studies reviewed in this chapter reveal that approaches to teaching English to anglophone Caribbean students are premised on whether their vernacular is viewed as a dialect of English or a separate language. I review studies of educational responses to linguistic diversity in England, Canada, and the United States, paying particular attention to the ways in which language attitudes affect pedagogy. I also discuss the challenges of teaching standard academic English to Creole English-speaking students and of socializing them to various models of literacies, in particular to what Scollon and Scollon (1981) call "essayist literacy," the register that is typically privileged in school. Finally, there is a review of the studies on the characteristics of spoken and written (essayist) language and the features of Caribbean Creole English.

Chapter 4 describes the site of the study, the criteria used for selecting the four participants, and the methods used to document and analyze their language and educational experiences. I then show how salient features of essayist writing and Creole English are used as a heuristic tool for analyzing the participants' writing.

The next four chapters constitute the core of the study. A detailed narrative of each of the two Guyanese and two Jamaican participants respectively describes his/her linguistic and educational experiences in the home country and in New York City. I discuss each participant's views of his/her own language use, actual linguistic behavior, language attitudes, and educational experiences from primary school to college. Samples of their college writing are provided and analyzed on discourse and morphosyntactic levels.

The concluding chapter discusses my findings and makes connections to speakers of other nonstandard languages such as African-American Vernacular English. Finally, I reiterate the importance of language attitudes in education and suggest a language policy that I believe responds appropriately to the issues raised in the study.

2

Creoles, Identity, and Caribbean Migration

CARIBBEAN ENGLISH-BASED CREOLES

Linguist Lawrence Carrington (1992) asserts that the term "English-speaking" is an inexactitude with regard to the anglophone Caribbean, for although English is the official language in the region, the mass vernacular is some variety of English-based Creole. Creole languages emerged from a unique language contact situation that was a direct result of European colonial expansion in the Caribbean between 1500 and 1900 (Bickerton, 1981). The plantation systems established during this period were mostly engaged in monoculture, usually sugar—a crop that demanded a large, sustained labor force. This need resulted in the importation of a large mass of mainly non-European laborers drawn from different language groups who were forced to coexist with a ruling European minority in rigidly stratified societies. The labor force consisted mostly of slaves from West Africa, later supplemented by indentured laborers from India, China, and Portugal. It is generally assumed that these various language groups evolved some form of an auxiliary contact language, native to none of them, known as a "pidgin," and that this language, suitably expanded, became the native or "Creole" language of the Caribbean communities that exist today.

Creoles are in most cases different enough from languages in the original contact situation to be considered "new" languages. Their phonology, morphology, and syntax are akin to those of some West African languages such as Twi or Ewe, and their lexicons are mainly drawn from the dominant European language. In the case of the anglophone Caribbean, Creoles bear a superficial resemblance to English because of their English-dominant lexicon—hence the term "Creole-Englishes." It is this quasi-relation to English, however, that has precluded Creoles from being considered separate languages, often giving them pejorative names such as "bad" or "broken" English.

The Creole Continuum

Historically, Creoles in the anglophone Caribbean have not enjoyed autonomy as languages in their own right (Winford, 1994). The history of slavery and British colonization in the Caribbean has forced the continued interaction of standard English and Creoles in a lopsided arrangement that has privileged the standard variety and stigmatized Creoles. The interaction of the two language varieties has created what DeCamp (1971) calls a *Creole Continuum*. The basic premise of the continuum is that there is no sharp cleavage between the Creole and standard English. Rather, there is a continuous spectrum of speech varieties ranging from the *basilect* (the most conservative Creole) to the *mesolect* (mid-range, less creolized varieties) to the *acrolect* (the standard variety, with some local phonological and lexical features). In strictly linguistic terms, it is the basilect that is the true Creole and the mesolect is referred to as *Creole English* (Roberts, 1988).

Generally speaking, there is a correlation between low social status and basilectal speech, and conversely, high social status and acrolectal speech. This is not, however, an absolute phenomenon. Winford (1994) notes that social status alone does not account for language use. Education, ethnicity, and rural/urban provenance are all factors that affect one's speech. For example, Rickford's (1987) study of the language patterns among working-class estate and middle-class nonestate workers in Guyana shows a strong correlation between rural provenance and basilectal speech. His study also indicates that the majority of rural residents whose speech is typically basilectal are of East Indian descent. On the other hand, the bulk of Guyana's upper-middle class is concentrated in Georgetown, the capital, and the most prestigious schools are located there. It is no surprise that residents in Georgetown are generally better educated, mesolect- or acrolect-dominant speakers.

There is also a fair amount of style shifting along the continuum as the need arises to adjust to social context. Basilectal to mesolectal varieties are preferred for intimates, humor, and informal situations. Acrolectal speech is generally reserved for school, church, business, and other formal domains. These patterns of linguistic behavior are not mutually exclusive as there is often overlap in speech varieties. Furthermore, style shifting along the continuum is often bidirectional, as Caribbean natives engage in "acts of identity," revealing through their use of language both their personal identity and sense of social and ethnic solidarity and difference (LePage & Tabouret-Keller, 1985).

Creole English, Education, and Identity

For most of the post-emancipation period in the Caribbean until the colonies were granted independence, one's social status was clearly identified among other factors by the degree to which one's speech approximated or deviated from the acrolect. This phenomenon was reinforced by an education system whose sole medium of instruction was standard English and flatly denied any validity to Creole English, the mass vernacular. Colonial education, therefore, reflected and reinforced the rigid social stratification of Caribbean societies, and language was its most palpable manifestation.

As Caribbean countries approached independence, political and structural changes began to take place that had a profound impact on the linguistic situation there. The thirst for self-government, characterized by a strong anti-imperialist stance, led to a greater drive towards self-assertion (Christie, 1983). Caribbean people worked fervently to replace "the old striving towards vague, foreign ideals which, more often than not, led to the rejection of self and with it a rejection of the vernacular" (pp. 208-209). Thus, the immediate pre- and post-independence periods were marked by the widespread use of Creole English as an affirmation of national and ethnic pride and as the language of true Caribbean identity. At the same time, masses of Creole English-dominant speakers began to gain access to schooling beyond the primary level, as part of the restructuring of the education system (Devonish, 1986).

With the entry of the Creole English-speaking masses into the education system, a contradiction has emerged. Although access to education for all social classes is seen as necessary for building a productive work force in developing Caribbean nations, education continues to be conducted in standard English, the language of the minority elite. Furthermore, social mobility is still premised on the mastery of standard English. There is, then, an ongoing tension between public attitudes that elevate standard English over Creole English and private attitudes that express pride in Creole English (Winford, 1994). This contradictory linguistic situation still exists today and has produced what Morgan (1994) calls "competing identities and language policies" (p. 1) where there is a simultaneous celebration of that which is creole and colonial. Still, the tangible rewards of identifying with the language of the colonial master are alluring. Thus, although the majority of anglophone Caribbean natives actually speak Creole or some variety of Creole English, they continue to label their language as "English," at least in public domains, for Creole is associated with low racial, social, political, and economic status (Winer, 1993). Caribbean people live and ultimately migrate with this dual (Creole/English) linguistic identity.

ANGLOPHONE CARIBBEAN MIGRATION

The most important factor ushering the massive new immigration into the United States was the Hart-Cellar Immigration Reform Act of 1965, which abandoned the national origins quota system favoring Northern and Western Europeans (Foner, 1987; Palmer, 1995). Natives of English-speaking Caribbean countries, who had been subject to very small quotas, were then included in the 120,000 ceiling for the Western Hemisphere (South and North America and the Caribbean). Congress established uniform limits of 20,000 immigrants per country. This reform proved a boon for anglophone Caribbean natives, for as more Caribbean territories became independent nations after 1962, more and more Caribbean natives became eligible to immigrate. Furthermore, one important aspect of the 1965 Act was the encouragement of family reunification whereby immigrants could sponsor close relatives at home. Thus, as the number of immigrants in the United States started to grow, the number of people in the Caribbean that they were eligible to sponsor increased dramatically. It comes as no surprise, then, that in the 10 years after the Act went into effect, anglophone Caribbean migration exceeded that of the previous 70 years. Moreover, the numbers continued to grow in the following decades. According to Kasinitz (1992) "[b]y the early 1980s approximately 50,000 legal immigrants from the anglophone Caribbean and another 6,000 to 8,000 from Haiti were entering the United States annually. Approximately half of these people settled in New York City" (p. 27). Although the United States Immigration Act might be considered the primary "pull" factor that drew Caribbean natives to the New York, "push" factors in the Caribbean helped to propel migration. As Kasinitz (1992) notes, "high unemployment and limited options in these small countries make emigration often the only viable option even for members of the middle class" (p. 29).

Another noteworthy feature of the 1965 Act was that it gave preference to professional and skilled workers (Bonnett, 1981). Therefore, in the post-1965 years up until the late 1970s, the United States attracted Caribbean immigrants who were generally middle class, better educated, and skilled. This drastic "brain drain" left a dearth of professionals (including teachers) and skilled personnel in the Caribbean. The exodus of such a significant portion of the middle class meant that masses of mostly poor and working-class, basilectal speakers were left behind in floundering education systems.

As the 1980s approached, conditions worsened. Economic stagnation, political instability, and a general social demise in the Caribbean forced unprecedented numbers of people to flee their countries. Migration continued to increase, this time dominated by large sections of the underclass, who were predominantly basilectal Creole speakers with minimum proficiency in standard English. New York City has been the primary destination of these recent immigrants, Guyanese and Jamaicans being foremost among them.

Citing statistics from the Immigration and Naturalization Service (INS), Rivera-Batiz (1994) shows that between 1982 and 1991, Jamaica led the anglophone Caribbean in terms of legal migration to New York City followed by Guyana. In Table 1 on the following page, Rivera-Batiz lists the number of legal immigrants moving to New York City between 1982 and 1991 based on INS data. Anglophone Caribbean countries are marked with an asterisk.

The statistics show that of the 898,213 new legal immigrants in New York City between 1982 and 1991, the four anglophone Caribbean countries taken together account for a total of 183,633 or approximately 20 percent. These are significant figures given that the population of Guyana, for example, is less than one million. Furthermore, the INS estimates that an additional 21,200 and 10,900 illegal immigrants came from Jamaica and Guyana respectively during the same period. In an article by Dugger (1997) showing recent statistics released by the New York City Department of Planning, we see that although the numbers have dropped slightly, Jamaica and Guyana continue to lead the anglophone Caribbean in terms of migration. These two countries have been surpassed only by the Dominican Republic, the Former Soviet Union, and China. Between 1990 and 1994, the Department of Planning reports 32,918 Jamaicans and 30,764 Guyanese legally migrated to New York City.

These statistics translate directly to public school and college enrollment. Between 1989 and 1992, 10,000 Jamaicans enrolled in New York City public schools followed by 7,000 Guyanese (Rivera-Batiz, 1994). At Long Island University in Brooklyn, New York, the site of this study, the statistics are also consistent. Of the 128 anglophone Caribbean students reg-

Table 1. Legal Immigrants Moving to New York City From 1982 to 1991.

Country of Origin	Immigrants	Country of Origin	Immigrants
Dominican Republic	151,712	Hong Kong	13,737
Jamaica*	87,112	Poland	12,712
China	79,841	Honduras	11,381
Guyana*	67,729	Britain	11,054
Haiti	48,518	Israel	10,073
Soviet Union	36,593	Peru	9,920
Colombia	26,834	Pakistan	9,803
India	24,938	El Salvador	9,689
Korea	24,361	Barbados*	9,450
Ecuador	22,857	Bangladesh	8,695
Philippines	19,791	Ireland	7,321
Trinidad & Tobago*	19,342		
Total			898,213

Source: New York City Department of City Planning (1993)

istered in writing classes during the spring 1996 semester, Jamaicans and Guyanese constituted the majority—47 Jamaicans and 35 Guyanese.

The language and academic preparation of these newly arrived immigrant students are radically unlike those of their predecessors. Whereas earlier Caribbean immigrants were more uniform in their academic preparation and demonstrated greater proficiency in standard English, newly arrived immigrants show a kind of schism in academic preparation. Some are moderately prepared, but many are poorly schooled, reflecting the unstable educational situation in the Caribbean. Furthermore, their predominantly basilectal-mesolectal speech has called their "English-speaking" classification into question. For the first time, educators have been forced to decide whether Caribbean Creole Englishes constitute separate languages or should be considered dialects of English.

3

Languages, Dialects and Education

CREOLES: LANGUAGES OR DIALECTS?

Whether Creoles are languages in their own right or merely dialects of English is more than a linguistic question. As Winford (1994) contends, "the autonomy of a language variety is not solely, or even primarily, a linguistic question, but also involves considerations of political, sociocultural and historical factors" (p. 45). The fact is that Caribbean Creole Englishes are in an anomalous position where they are in constant interaction with a prestige variety of standard English; hence, their autonomy as languages is continually challenged. Alleyne (1987) notes that such Creoles are not well-defined linguistic systems and therefore defy clearcut definitions as either languages or dialects. He resolves the issue by returning to the concept of the creole continuum. If pressed, however, most linguists tend to favor the view of Creoles as languages in their own right. Studies have shown that wherever Creoles are viewed as autonomous languages, they enjoy high prestige (Alleyne, 1980; Winford, 1994) and conversely, where viewed as dialects, they are stigmatized.

Winford (1994) argues that where Creoles coexist with quite unrelated official languages, as in Surinam or the Dutch Antilles, their linguistic or sociopolitical status is never called into question. It is generally accepted that Creoles in such situations constitute separate linguistic systems, and no known attempt has been made to treat them as dialects of the European languages to which they are lexically related. He asserts that

> as far as their sociopolitical status is concerned, while they do not stand in egalitarian relationship with the official language, they generally enjoy more prestige than those Creoles that are part of a continuum. (p. 45)

In his comparative study of the languages of diasporic Africans in the Americas and the Caribbean, Alleyne (1980) points out that a very different scenario obtains in continuum situations. He states,

> [l]inguistic forms which are used in relatively homogenous structures in Surinam or even in rural peasant communities in Jamaica, and are there positively functional, become dysfunctional when involved in variation patterns with standard forms of speech. (p. 19)

In other words, when Creoles are juxtaposed and interact with a European-derived standard language viewed as the ideal norm in the same socioeconomic environment, as is the case with most Creoles outside of isolated rural communities, they come to be viewed as deformed versions of the standard and are negatively evaluated. Ironically, some of the most negative views of Creole Englishes are held by the very speakers of these languages.

Implications for Pedagogy

Most pedagogical approaches to teaching Caribbean Creole speakers are premised on whether Creole Englishes are to be viewed as languages or dialects. In his study of Caribbean and African languages and students in England, Dalphinis (1985) underscores the challenge of teaching standard English to Caribbean students in schools that are at once the major locus of contact between Creole English and standard English *and* the guardians of standard English. In such an environment, Creole Englishes are likely to be stigmatized.

Dalphinis examines the arguments for and against English as a Second Language (ESL) approaches to teaching standard English to Caribbean students. The most forceful argument against an ESL approach is the claim that Caribbean students speak a dialect of English and as such have no need for ESL. Another argument against ESL is that any special linguistic treatment of Caribbean students may place an undue emphasis on their home language, when what is really needed is intensive immersion in standard English (SE), the language students need for academic achievement and upward mobility.

The main linguistic argument in favor of ESL approaches with Caribbean students is the judgment that they are bilinguals who speak a language distinctly different from standard English. It is also argued that an ESL perspective would heighten contrasts between the SE target language and Creole English through contrastive analysis and error analysis. Greater awareness of contrasts between the two languages will result in greater control over both. Furthermore, it is argued that recognition of Creoles as languages rather than dialects of English would diminish the alienation of Caribbean students.

Dalphinis himself argues in favor of Creoles as autonomous languages. He notes that Creoles have also been viewed as prolonged interlanguages, and in this regard, Caribbean students would benefit from ESL approaches that would "facilitate learning contexts for the changing of interlanguage Caribbean language forms into their SE targets" (pp. 195-196).

In her research on teaching literacy to Creole speakers in Jamaica, Thompson (1984) states that Schumann also compared Creoles to fossilized interlanguages. Thompson argues, however, that

> the comparison is relevant and illuminating, but can only be partially applied. Whereas the interlanguage of the foreign language learner is a linguistic system used in addition to his native language, Creole is a native language which is adequate for everyday social needs. (p. 173)

It has crystallized into a full-fledged, rule-governed system, and the Creole-speaking learner has the ability to operate at several levels on the speech continuum. It is only when s/he becomes involved in a formal learning situation that any deficiency becomes apparent. Thompson asserts that the task of the teacher is to assist students in acquiring the standard language as an additional linguistic code to be used for particular purposes and on specific occasions. Her work points to the failure of literacy programs based on the "native language approach"—the assumption that English, rather than Creole, is the first language of Jamaicans. In such programs, Creoles are either ignored, or at best, viewed as linguistic aberrations. Although some students succeed in these programs, Thompson states that more than half of them experience severe reading and writing difficulties.

In a study of newly arrived Caribbean students in New York City public schools, Narvaez and Garcia (1992) note that defining the language of these students is a challenge for New York City school officials. The language of new Caribbean immigrants ranges from basilects to varieties of Creole English to standard Caribbean English. Many teachers cannot understand basilectal speakers and this often leads to their placement in ESL classes. At the same time, students who speak Creole English as their primary language and are under the mistaken belief that they speak standard English are baffled and frustrated when they are assigned to ESL classes that are inappropriate for them. Because of the constant interaction of Creole English and standard English along the continuum, Creole English speakers' receptive knowledge of standard English far exceeds that of "true" non-native speakers of English; hence, traditional ESL classes do not address their linguistic needs. Furthermore, because Caribbean Creole English-speaking students perceive themselves as native *speakers* of standard English, they may have little motivation to frame themselves as *learners* of standard English under the conditions of traditional ESL classes. Such students are best served in regular English classes with teachers who are appropriately trained to address their linguistic needs.

Educators of Caribbean students are therefore challenged to find alternative approaches to teaching standard English to Creole English speakers. In individual Caribbean countries, where there is some degree of similarity among the speech varieties spoken by students, the linguistic environment is more conducive to designing a fairly uniform language curriculum. However, in North America and England, where educators encounter a wide range of Caribbean students from various countries, socioeconomic, educational, and linguistic backgrounds, the task is more formidable. The following section examines how educators in England, Canada, and the United States have responded to linguistic diversity with particular attention to Caribbean students.

ANGLOPHONE CARIBBEAN STUDENTS IN ENGLAND

The United Kingdom has been the pioneer in research on Caribbean students primarily because of its long history of colonial ties with the anglophone Caribbean. In addition, the United Kingdom actively recruited Caribbean immigrants to replenish its labor force following World War II. The Caribbean men and women who migrated to England in the post-war period settled there, and the language of their offspring presented a major linguistic challenge to modern British educators. In 1977, the Committee of Inquiry into the Education of Children from Ethnic Minority Groups focused their attention on the Caribbean community in England. The committee expressed concern about the poor performance of Caribbean students in British schools and recommended a high-level independent inquiry into the cause of underachievement of Caribbean students. After two years of probing among educators and Caribbean immigrants themselves, the committee, chaired by Anthony Rampton, released its report. Among the many factors cited as major contributors to Caribbean underachievement, linguistic difficulty was listed second in order of importance (racism being the first).

In research on the language of Caribbean students in England, Edwards (1983) points out that a recurring question is whether Caribbean Creoles should be classified as dialects of English or as separate languages. Unfortunately, the answer to this question has been largely left up to teachers with limited linguistic knowledge about the Caribbean and subtle ethnolinguistic biases. It comes as no surprise, then, that British teachers saw Caribbean Creole English speakers as linguistically deprived, because their language was arguably further removed from standard English than any British dialect.

Edwards and Redfern (1992) note that the early approach to Caribbean students was to view their educational needs as "exclusively linguistic and temporary." British educators adopted a kind of *laissez-faire* approach that was essentially assimilationist—teach standard English and the other problems will be solved. Over time, educators realized that the needs of Caribbean students were neither exclusively linguistic nor temporary. Caribbean underachievement persisted, and often Caribbean students were placed in schools for the "educationally subnormal," the implication being that standard English was "normal" and Creole English was "subnormal."

Having acknowledged the failure of the assimilationist approach, British educators embarked on a policy of *compensatory education*—an attempt to "compensate" for the so-called "linguistic deficit" of Caribbean students by providing separate, intense language training for them. Compensatory education, premised as it was on a deficit model, also failed to meet the needs of Caribbean students. It perpetuated a pathological framework whereby linguistic minority students were seen as having problems that could only be resolved through intensive English teaching in isolation from the mainstream.

Eventually, British educators came to espouse a "difference" approach; that is, the language of Caribbean students was "different but not deficient." This new attitude emerged within a framework of changing educational responses to diversity. In a sociopolitical climate that was fast becoming one of cultural pluralism, British educators came to agree that minority students should be encouraged to develop their own linguistic and cultural resources within the school.

ANGLOPHONE CARIBBEAN STUDENTS IN CANADIAN SCHOOLS

In response to rapidly changing demographics in Canada, the Canadian government passed the Multiculturalism Act in 1988 (Edwards & Redfern, 1992). Despite the official policy of multiculturalism, the dominant teaching paradigm within Canadian classrooms has remained one of cultural assimilation. In such a climate, Caribbean students (being at once ethnic, racial, and linguistic minorities) have not fared well.

Studies by Anderson and Grant (1987), Coelho (1991), and Solomon (1992) have investigated the performance of Caribbean students in Canadian schools. Among the reasons cited by Anderson and Grant for academic underachievement were the linguistic difficulties experienced by Caribbean students. For one thing, Caribbean students who entered Canadian schools declared their mother tongue as English. Despite this fact, surveys have shown that 20 percent of ESL teachers in Canada report having Caribbean students in their classes. Clearly, the language of Caribbean students was an anomaly for Canadian educators as it was for British educators, and the students' unique linguistic situation consequently affected placement decisions. After persistent complaints by both Caribbean students and their parents about students being (mis)placed into ESL classes, Canadian educators came to recognize the inappropriateness of ESL classes for Caribbean Creole English speakers.

Canadian schools subsequently introduced a new language program called Standard English as a Second Dialect (SESD), specifically designed for Caribbean Creole English-speaking students. Coelho (1991) notes that the primary assumption of the SESD program is that "Creole speakers have needs different from those of students of English as a Second Language, and different from those of native speakers of standard English" (p. 43). Three curriculum objectives for this language program are identified: linguistic, affective, and cognitive. Based on her study of anglophone Caribbean students in Canadian schools, Coelho concludes that because these students do not perceive themselves as language learners, they may never attend to some features of the standard variety of the language in the way that ESL students typically do. Therefore, the linguistic component of a SESD program has to include three different kinds of objectives:

> Objectives related to acquisition of the grammatical forms, sound system and vocabulary of Standard English, functional objectives related to how to carry out specific intentions in verbal interactions in a wide range of social contexts, and objectives related to assisting students to perceive themselves as language learners without damage to self-esteem. (p. 57)

In terms of affective objectives, Coelho suggests that teachers

> select instructional strategies, curriculum content, and learning materials which will support students in developing the positive [racial and cultural] self-image and interpersonal skills necessary for academic and social success. (p. 62)

Cognitive objectives should challenge the underlying assumptions in much curriculum design and curriculum should be changed to reflect the diverse experiences students bring to school.

Gopaul-McNicol (1993) states that SESD classes, in principle, seem to address the needs of Creole English speakers, because they allow Caribbean students to speak the vernacular, providing considerable opportunity for oral expression. Students are gradually guided toward productive control of the mainstream dialect. One of the main drawbacks of these classes, however, is the fact that they are taught by mainstream teachers who are not Creole English speakers; thus, there is a lack of familiarity with the students' language and culture. The problem is compounded by the shortage of Caribbean teachers in Canadian schools. Gopaul-McNicol suggests that Caribbean students might be helped by what she calls "Supplementary Instruction in the English Language" (p. 86). However, such a program, like all other forms of supplementary instruction, requires both political will and institutional and financial commitment, which may not be forthcoming in difficult economic times. In the final analysis, Solomon (1992) suggests that any significant improvement in the schooling of Caribbean students must incorporate strategies that address the structure, culture, and politics of schooling.

ANGLOPHONE CARIBBEAN STUDENTS IN AMERICAN SCHOOLS

Prior to the arrival of the latest influx of immigrants, very little attention was paid to Caribbean immigrants as a group in the United States. This was because Caribbean immigrants, until recently, fared well in the United States because of what Bonnett (1981) calls their "migrant ideology of hard saving and investment" (p. 5). But, as mentioned earlier, newly arrived immigrants are generally less equipped for success in American workplaces or schools due to their academic underpreparation.

Traditionally, American educators have used various terms to refer to Caribbean Creole Englishes: "dialect," "broken English," and so forth. Occasionally, the language of Caribbean immigrants has been loosely referred to as "Black English" (hereafter called African American Vernacular English, AAVE)—a language mainly spoken by African Americans that, according to Dillard (1972), can be traced to a "creolized version of English based upon a pidgin spoken by slaves" (p. 6). From a linguistic perspective, the label "Black English" is a misnomer, for the language of Caribbean basilectal and mesolectal speakers exhibit far more "creole" features than that of speakers of AAVE. Although Caribbean Creole Englishes (CCE) do share some morphosyntactic features with AAVE (for example, zero copula or zero inflection for tense, subject/verb agreement, and plurals), they have not undergone the extensive decreolization that AAVE has, the latter being more heavily influenced by the preponderance of standard language speakers in the United States in contrast to the Creole English-speaking majority in the Caribbean.

From an educator's perspective, however, CCE and AAVE speakers are similar enough to be classified as one type. Thus, CCE and AAVE speakers, as well as other students whose dialects are at variance with standard English and who exhibit poor to mediocre writing skills, are usually assigned to the same developmental writing classes. Caribbean students, for whom "English is neither a native language nor a foreign language" (Craig, 1971, p. 376), are particularly vulnerable to linguistic misclassification. For example, in her study of Jamaican Creole English-speaking students in New York City public schools, Pratt-Johnson (1993) notes that on entering school, these students are usually faced with one of three possibilities: (a) if their language seems decidedly creolized, they are assigned to ESL classes; (b) because they are labeled officially English-speaking, they are offered no special services; or (c) they are assigned to special education classes with the assumption that the smaller class size and slower pace will solve their "problems." Whichever option is chosen, Caribbean students find themselves in an unfavorable position, because their linguistic needs are mishandled or go unchecked. When this is coupled with the deficit these new immigrants suffer in basic schooling, one is not surprised that Sontag (1992) describes many of them as floundering or "misplaced in special education classes or left on their own to sink or swim in the mainstream" (p. 22).

Only in recent times have American educators acknowledged that the language of Caribbean students merits special attention. In isolated cases across the country, educators are grappling with the issue. For example, at Evanston Township High School in Illinois, the Caribbean Academic Program, financed mostly by a government grant, offers a language-based instruction program to Caribbean students stressing the syntactical differences between Creole English and standard English (Sontag, 1992). However, the situation of Caribbean students is primarily a New York City debate because an overwhelming majority of Caribbean immigrants have settled in that city. In the absence of governmental funding (students from the officially English-speaking Caribbean are not legally entitled to ESL or bilingual education), local educators have been scraping together improvised programs to help Caribbean students. *Project Omega*, a five-year-old transition program for Caribbean immigrants at four Brooklyn high schools, is financed by the shrinking budget of the superintendent of Brooklyn high schools.

In two Brooklyn schools, a nongraded program for elementary students, the *Transition Institute*, has been established under the supervision of the Caribbean Research Center at Medgar Evers College. The Center has been proactive in its focus on Caribbean students. According to Irish (1997), the Center has published a number of texts and manuals as a resource base to assist teachers in New York working with Caribbean students. In addition, it offers

> a vibrant and effective professional development program [including an annual summer institute] geared to enhance teachers' sensitivity to cultural diversity, as well as a research and teacher-support program in curriculum and assessment that draws on Caribbean resources. (p. 5)

The Center also offers the Parent Empowerment Program (PEP) to encourage parent involvement as part of its agenda for community empowerment.

The most significant effort thus far to address the needs of Caribbean students was a vote by the New York State Board of Regents to send the legislature a proposal to finance a $600,000 pilot program for immigrant students from the nineteen Caribbean countries where English is the official language. Caribbean students who are supposed to be "English-speaking" are not perceived by many educators as speaking "English," at least not a variety that is compatible with academic norms. At a recent conference of Caribbean educators in Tarrytown, New York, one educator (in referring to Caribbean students) remarked, "Let's redefine them as nonnative speakers of English so we can get some funding" (Sontag, 1992, p. 22). The comment is politically motivated but misses the mark. It is clear that Caribbean Creole English speakers defy clearcut linguistic classification, and therefore pedagogical practices in regard to these students must take into account their unique linguistic situation. Winer (1993) suggests a broad-based approach—one that includes knowledge of Caribbean students' language and culture. Teachers should be aware of the structure and validity of Creole Englishes and of their unique relationship to standard English. London (1980) suggests that teachers of Caribbean students will require among other support systems a sense of Caribbean history and a sensitivity towards the backgrounds of students, their values and culture patterns, their environment and the specific influences which impinge upon them. (p. 11)

He also emphasizes the need for teachers to develop a sensitivity towards non-American phenomena, including speech patterns which may be different but not necessarily incorrect, and British-oriented spelling and writing style which, he believes, "will gradually be adapted to the American mode" (p. 12).

LITERACIES AND WRITING IN AN AMERICAN CONTEXT

London's assumption that the Caribbean student's writing will eventually be adapted to the "American mode" presupposes a process of linguistic acculturation over time towards what might be considered appropriate writing and literacy practices in an American context. I would argue that London's assumption cannot be assumed to hold true for all Caribbean students. The degree to which a particular student successfully acculturates to American literacy practices depends on the student's educational experiences in the Caribbean and his/her desire and/or ability to adapt to such practices. The Caribbean immigrant student must also be able to figure out the underlying assumptions about literacy practices in American society and how these assumptions are enacted in the college classroom.

Two models of literacy have dominated American culture: (a) The *autonomous model*, which views literacy as an individual skill acquired through formal schooling, utilizing oral language as a basis and ultimately affecting cognitive development (McKay, 1996); (b) the *sociocultural model*, which, according to Schieffelin and Cochran-Smith (1984), focuses primarily on "literacy as a social and cultural phenomenon, something that exists between people and something that connects individuals to a range of experiences and to different points in time" (p. 4). Street (1991) has been one of the chief proponents of the latter model, for he feels it recognizes a multiplicity of literacies in which "the meaning and uses of literacy practices are related to specific cultural contexts" (p. 1).

The two models need not be mutually exclusive, for the particular skills learned through either one should be able to be applied to the other. In reality, however, the autonomous model is not only acquired through formal schooling, but has sought to separate (and privilege) the skills learned in formal schooling from those learned through other human experiences. It has also perpetuated the "great divide" between oral and written language. Street (1991) criticizes the two basic principles of this model: first, that oral and written language are radically different and secondly, that literacy, in and of itself, leads to certain predictable forms of cognitive development. In fact, he believes that the "great divide" between oral and written language has been exaggerated because the uses made of written language in some cultures can be easily handled by oral language in others.

It should be noted that the "great divide" is not between oral and written language per se, but between a particular kind of oral language (the casual conversations and narratives of day-to-day communicative activities or of those who are less formally schooled, referred to by Cummins [1984] as Basic Interpersonal Communication Skills [BICS]) and a particular kind of written language, acquired through formal schooling, referred to by Cummins (1984) as Cognitive Academic Language Proficiency (CALP) or by Olson (1977b) as "literate prose" (p. 65). This kind of written language is produced within a broader register that Scollon and Scollon (1981) have termed "essayist literacy." Olson (1977a) argues that essayist literacy was the last stage in a progression of significant events in the Western linguistic tradition, beginning with the invention of alphabetic writing, then the development of explicitness at the semantic level, followed by the arrival of the printing press, and finally the rise of the British essayist technique. Farr (1993) states that "a number of genres, both oral and written, exist within this register, for example, school essays, instructional lectures, oral reports, research papers and textbooks" (p. 8). Because essayist literacy is generally associated with academic situations—the context within which this study is conducted—it is necessary to pause and highlight some of the most recognizable stylistic features of this register. Various scholars of literacy (Ong, 1977; Scollon and Scollon, 1981; Walters, 1994) have identified the prominent characteristics of essayist literacy as follows:

1. The ability to read and write decontextualized material
2. Removal of traces of authorship; fictionalization of audience
3. Idealized reader and writer
4. Writing removed from an actual situation
5. Emphasis on internally logical text, especially explicit marking of logical connections among propositions (or sentences)
6. Use of standard spelling and phonology; hypotactic syntax; attention to conventions of grammatical correctness
7. Presenting information using specific cohesive strategies and providing careful analysis and evidence for claims made.

When scholars like Halliday (1989) and Chafe and Danielewicz (1987) refer to the differences between oral and written language, they are, in fact, underscoring (although not explicitly) the differences between nonessayist oral language (the kind of language many students typically bring to school) and essayist writing as characterized by the features mentioned above.

Halliday (1989), unlike Street (1991), believes that writing and speaking are not just alternative ways of doing the same thing; rather, they are ways of doing different things, as evidenced by their distinctive characteristics. Halliday states that written language is dense, represents phenomena as products, and creates a more static view of the world. Because some of the primary functions of written language are to name, to conceptualize, and to provide stability of information, it displays a high ratio of *lexical density* (the number of lexical items per clause) and nominalization. Furthermore, because written language is not anchored in the here and now, it requires a high level of verbal explicitness. Additionally, Halliday argues that one major difference between written and oral language is lexical density.

Halliday claims that oral language, by contrast, is anchored in the here and now; hence, there is less need for verbal explicitness. Most of the meaning in oral language is negotiated in context. The speaker's state of mind, emotions, facial gestures, as well as prosodic features such as intonation, rhythm, and tonic prominence combine to make meaning. Oral language is sparse but grammatically intricate. It represents phenomena as processes, so that there is a tendency to describe things as happening by frequently using verbs of action and feeling such as *make, do, eat, want, feel*.

Chafe and Danielewicz (1987), like Halliday, also distinguish between properties of oral and written language. They argue that written language shows a greater range of vocabulary than oral language because in writing there is more time to plan and explore a variety of lexical choices. Chafe and Danielewicz therefore expand on the notion of lexical density by not only accounting for the number of lexical items but also the number of *different* items in a text, a phenomenon known as the *type/token ratio*. The type/token ratio is the number of different words in a sample divided by the total number of words.

Just as Halliday notes that most of the meaning in oral language is negotiated in context aided by prosodic features, Chafe and Danielewicz also note what they call a high level of *involvement* of self in oral language, reinforced by frequent references to concrete persons, actions, space, and time. They contrast the *involvement* of oral language with the *detachment* of written language. Detached language uses clauses whose subjects refer to abstractions; it also tends to utilize more passive constructions.

Chafe and Danielewicz are careful to point out that oral and written language do not form a simple dichotomy. There are many instances where speakers borrow from a written lexicon and vice versa. For example, academic lectures are more literary than casual conversations, and letters more conversational than academic papers. They claim that letters fall somewhere between oral and written language, for they display a high level of personal involvement while taking advantage of the deliberateness that writing allows. Here, Chafe and Danielewicz are reiterating Farr's (1993) point that the oral/written issue is really one of register.

Halliday emphasizes another fundamental difference between speech and writing: speaking and listening come naturally; reading and writing must be taught and have come to be associated with educated practice. He suggests that the educated or literate adult understands the difference between (nonessayist) oral and (essayist) written language and is able to use them in socially appropriate ways, for in practice, speech and writing are used in different contexts for different purposes though with some overlap (words in parentheses are my emphasis).

For many Caribbean and African-American students whose cultures are steeped in an oral tradition, the oral/written divide is one of their biggest challenges upon entering a formal schooling environment. It should be pointed out that Caribbean Creole English is as actively discouraged in most Caribbean schools as African-American Vernacular English is in most American schools. Therefore, when Caribbean and African-American students come to college—one of the principal custodians of the "great divide" theory—their oral language skills (BICS) are often subordinated to the focus on mastering CALP or conventions of essayist literacy, especially in writing.

It is difficult for students who are unfamiliar with this register to become proficient in it when, as Walters (1994) notes, "schools rarely, if ever, explicitly teach the patterns of language use associated with academic discourse or essayist literacy" (p. 642). Yet, there is a tacit assumption that by the time students are about to enter college they should already "know how to write," that is, demonstrate the requisite proficiency in essayist literacy. This assumption has real consequences for students because mastering essayist literacy is used as the benchmark for admission to and success in college; thus, it serves an essentially gatekeeping function. The four student participants in this study were all categorized as "basic writers" on entering college because their writing on the placement test missed the mark; that is, their writing did not demonstrate a minimally acceptable level of skills in essayist literacy.

Bizzell (1984) argues that the entry of such basic writers into college not only precipitates a clash of dialects and discourse forms but also of worldviews. She states,

> [l]ike any other language community, the academic community uses a preferred dialect (so-called standard English) in a convention-bound discourse (academic discourse) that creates and organizes the knowledge that constitutes the community's world view. (p. 7)

Bizzell, citing Perry, characterizes the academic world view as one where there are no absolutes, where one must constantly (re)examine one's assumptions, think about one's own thoughts and compare these thoughts with those of others. One's views, choices and conclusions, therefore, are based on careful analysis, deliberation. and examination of evidence.

Academic writing reflects and reinforces this world view. It charges students to take a certain distance, to play with ideas at varying levels of abstraction, and to build an argument by compelling evidence through a complex apparatus of conventions. Ballard and Clanchy (1991) reinforce this point of view by arguing that in a Western university the development of a written argument is typically expected to conform to four criteria reflecting an analytic or speculative mode of learning. "It should be clearly focused, be the result of a wide and critical reading, present a reasoned argument, and be competently presented" (p. 30).

Gee (1990) would describe the worldview and behaviors practiced in academia as one type of *Discourse* (with a capital "D") reflected in and reinforced by *discourse* (with a small "d"). He defines Discourse as

> ways of behaving, interacting, valuing, thinking, believing, speaking and often reading and writing that are accepted as instantiations of particular roles by specific groups of people . . . [t]hey are always and everywhere social. (p. xix)

By way of contrast, he defines *discourse* as "connected stretches of language that make sense like conversations, stories, reports, arguments and essays" (p. 142). Gee theorizes that we develop primary Discourses through our families and we acquire secondary Discourses by apprenticeship to social institutions such as church, workplace, and school. The basic writer's task in academia, then, is two-fold: first, s/he must become apprenticed to the Discourse of school, in particular the college classroom; that is to say, s/he must think, value and behave like a college student—a daunting experience if academic Discourse is in conflict with his/her primary Discourse or if there is simply no opportunity to reinforce it outside of school. Secondly, s/he must learn and refine time-honored academic discourse conventions that include rhetorical matters of argumentation, organization, development, elaboration, style, purpose, and audience; syntactic issues such as sentence structure, word order, and prescriptive grammar rules; and other conventions such as punctuation, spelling, documentation and editing.

In the case of Caribbean Creole English-speaking students, mastery of academic discourse conventions might be challenging given that the rules of Creole English are decidedly different from those of academic discourse. As noted earlier, the students acquire school-based literacies in a language that they do not habitually speak; thus, the degree to which they become proficient in standard written English would depend, among other factors, on their educational experiences as well as their exposure and opportunities to use standard English outside of school.

Caribbean Students' Writing

The Caribbean Creole English-speaking student in an American academic setting is, in a very real sense, negotiating the Creole continuum in writing. At one end of the continuum is the student's language that s/he brings to school based on his/her sociocultural and educational experiences. At the other end is the standard written English of essayist literacy. The student's attempt to approximate standard written English often results in a kind of written academic *interlanguage*, borrowing Selinker's (1983) term. The interlanguage of the Caribbean Creole English-speaking student is a mixture of certain characteristics of Creole English and features of standard written English.

Roberts (1988) points out that the first notable characteristic of Creole English sentences is that they are *verb-centered* in contrast to standard written English, which distributes the semantic load of sentences over noun and verb phrases, adverbial and prepositional phrases:

> Creole English sentence: "Dey neva really use to do a lot o' writin' in 'igh school...jus' read a passage and fill in di blank."
> Standard English equivalent: "There was very little writing done in high school. We were simply asked to read a passage then fill in the blank."

Creole English sentences tend to involve more finite verbs and give greater flexibility to the functions of the verb. It is not surprising, therefore, that the outstanding features of Creole English syntax are directly related to the verb. Roberts notes that "since there are no inflections in the verb, meaning depends on the interrelationship of verb forms, and the relationship between the verb and other parts of the utterance, including context" (p. 63).

One of the best-known features of Creole English is what the observer might perceive as the absence of a copula: for example, *The man tall.* Roberts explains that in this example, the adjective is said to be functioning as the verb and predicate of the sentence and is called a *predicative adjective*, in which case no form of be is required. Sentences with predicative adjectives are universal in English-based Creoles and most other Creoles. Holm (1985) expands on this idea, noting that many African and Creole languages have distinct words for be depending on whether the predicate is a noun, adjective, prepositional phrase of location, and so forth. In Caribbean Creole English, zero copula is required if the predicate is a prepositional phrase of location or if forming the progressive tense. If the predicate is a noun, however, Creole English requires a form of be.

Other Creole English features include zero inflection for subject/verb concord, tense, verb participles, plurals, and possessives. Given that standard English requires conjugation of the verb to be as well as inflections, it is in these areas that the Creole English-speaking student is likely to exhibit first language transfer in his/her academic interlanguage.

In addition to the features mentioned above, Roberts discusses another feature of Creole English—sentence focus. He notes that in many of the world's languages there are two main ways of highlighting an element in a sentence—either in pronunciation by using heavier vocal stress or syntactically by putting the specific element in a prominent place in the sentence, usually at the beginning or at the end. Creole favors the syntactic method and usually puts the highlighted element at the beginning of a sentence, a phenomenon known as *front focusing* (Allsopp, 1979): for example, *My family, they don't talk like that.*

Roberts states that although standard English verbs such as go, does, done, been, did and had are the same form in Creole English, there are structural and semantic differences between the way these verbs are used in Creole English and the way they are used in standard English. For example, the so-called emphatic does in standard English is third person singular, is vocally stressed, and used in response to a contrary meaning or used with a negative (not), whereas in Creole English, does is unstressed, is used for any person/number, and denotes habitual action. He also asserts that Creole English words generally carry a greater functional load than standard English words. It was the expanded use of the word talking mentioned at the beginning of this study that caused the miscommunication between Charles and his instructor.

In terms of semantics, Winer (1993) notes that there are many "false friends" between Creole English and standard English: for example, miserable in Creole English means "badly behaved"; foot can refer to a larger part of the body, the toes to the hips; good night is used to initiate conversation as opposed to closing it in standard English. She contends that superficial similarities between Creole English and standard English yield positive results for Creole English speakers learning standard academic English in the beginning. But Winer cautions that "the Creole English speaker will reach crucial humps or plateaus at particular points and often be more frustrated and resentful than a typical ESL student" (p. 194). It is at these moments that writing teachers must demonstrate the most patience and sensitivity towards the unique linguistic situation of the Creole English speaker.

RESEARCH PERSPECTIVES

The review of the literature reveals that most of the research in regard to anglophone Caribbean students has focused on the grade school and high school levels and has generally addressed questions of pedagogical approaches based on whether the students' vernaculars are to viewed as autonomous languages or dialects of English. None of the studies discussed here has addressed the language of anglophone Caribbean students from the students' perspective nor has any study to date analyzed the writing of anglophone Caribbean students at the college level as they negotiate the "contact zone" (Pratt, 1995) between their Creole English and the English of the academy. This study seeks to broaden the scope of the research by posing two questions:

1. How do Caribbean immigrant students perceive their own language and schooling experiences in their home country and New York City?
2. What patterns emerge in the students' college writing with respect to (a) discourse features and (b) morphosyntactic features, and to what degree might these features be attributed to Creole influence?

4

The Study

SETTING

This qualitative study of four anglophone Caribbean students was conducted between 1994 and 1996 at the Brooklyn Campus of Long Island University (hereafter called LIU). LIU is a private university with three campuses—two on Long Island and one in downtown Brooklyn, New York. The Brooklyn Campus is located in the heart of a vibrant, multicultural community that includes thriving businesses and the borough hall. The Campus has a population of approximately 9,000 students who hail from a variety of ethnic, racial, and linguistic backgrounds. An estimated 60 percent of the students are of African descent, including African-Americans, Caribbeans, and continental Africans. The rest of the student population includes Latinos, Russians, and Asians. The vast majority of students are the first in their families to attend college. Many are single, working parents and almost all of them are supported by some kind of financial aid.

The Brooklyn Campus offered a two-semester long, 12-credit basic writing program that consisted of English 13 or 13X and English 14 or 14X (X denotes an ESL section), as well as a two-semester regular first-year composition sequence: English 16/16X and English 17/17X, each course worth three credits. Students were assigned to the basic writing program or the regular first-year composition sequence based on their performance on a placement test given by the administration, which combined both reading and writing (See Appendix A for sample placement test).

Each placement essay was read by two full-time faculty members from the English department, after which students were placed into classes based on their writing skills. Those who were deemed unprepared for regular first-year composition were placed into the first level of the basic writing program, English 13 or 13X. The remaining students were placed into first-year composition, English 16 or 16X. A small number of students failed the placement test and were recommended for a noncredit remedial writing course, Developmental Skills 10. Others who were beginner level ESL students were placed into the university's English Language Institute.

The writing program at LIU was modeled after the writing program at the University of Pittsburgh, with some adaptations to the local student population. The theoretical and pedagogical underpinnings of the program were firmly rooted in the notion that reading and writing are highly complex, interrelated processes. Students were taught to view writing as a recurrent process of reading, thinking, planning, pre-writing, drafting, rethinking, revising, rewriting, and editing. There was also a strong emphasis on teacher-student conferences and peer response to writing. In other words, "students were encouraged to view their writing as something that occurred not in isolation, but within a context of other writing, dialogue and exchange" (*LIU Handbook for Composition Teachers*, 1995, p. 9). Both formal and informal writing were important components of the program. Formal writing included drafted essays, in-class writing, and research papers. Informal writing included journal entries and free writing, which provided a forum for students to develop fluency by writing their thoughts without inhibition or concerns about correctness. Readings encompassed a wide range of genres including memoirs, fiction, poetry, critical essays, and newspaper articles. Students were encouraged to become critical readers and to view reading as an interpretive process where meanings do not simply reside in texts but are constructed through multiple perspectives.

In the basic writing sequence, English 13(X) and 14(X), the goal was for students to gain fluency in writing by engaging in intensive reading and writing about literary works and critical essays. English 13(X) and 14(X) were thematically organized and met six hours per week with a classroom instructor. In English 13(X) there were an additional four hours of writing workshops with an assigned workshop instructor, and in English 14(X) there were two hours of workshop. Students did a considerable amount of writing in these courses—formal writing, especially narrative, descriptive, and autobiographical essays, as well as in-class essays, journal writing, and free writing. Most of the assessment in these courses was carried out by a portfolio system. The writing portfolio is a representative sample of students' writing over a given period of time. Portfolios were collected and evaluated by the classroom and workshop instructors twice per semester, at midterm and at the end of the term. Students in English 13(X) who earned an "A" in the course might be allowed, at the instructor's discretion, to retake the placement test in an effort to be exempted from English 14(X).

On successful completion of the basic writing program, students were passed on to the regular two-semester-long first-year composition sequence. In the first semester course, English 16(X), students were expected to engage in more formal expository writing and to become proficient in rhetorical strategies of argumentation, persuasion, and so forth. Classes met for two-and-a-half hours per week, and there were no workshops, except in English 16X where there was a workshop that met once a week for one hour. Most readings were selected critical essays from multicultural anthologies, and writing assignments were usually related to the readings. The portfolio system of evaluation was also used in this course, the only difference being that the second reader is usually another English 16(X) instructor instead of a workshop instructor.[3] The last course in the sequence, English 17(X), focused on incorporating research into writing. Students explored primary and secondary sources in their research, which was usually thematically based. In the majority of classes, students did two or three short research papers on which most of their assessment was based or they did a semester-long oral history project.

PARTICIPANTS

The participants for the study were chosen from among a selected group of Guyanese and Jamaican students at LIU. The students all fit the profile of recent Caribbean immigrants; that is to say, they all migrated to New York City between 1985 and 1995. In addition, they were all placed into the basic writing program at LIU based on their performance on the placement test. All of the participants took English 13, 14, 16, and 17. For this study, I selected four participants—two Guyanese, Charles Benjamin and Myrna George, and two Jamaicans, Nadine Ferguson and Oscar Evans. The four participants represented a range of socioeconomic and educational backgrounds, reflecting the different types of anglophone Caribbean students that instructors might encounter in their classrooms. Charles and Myrna were both from rural, working-class families and migrated to the United States as teenagers.

Charles was a basilect-dominant speaker who was schooled entirely in a rural area and attended a nontraditional high school in Guyana. Myrna was a mesolect-dominant speaker who attended a rural primary school and a traditional academic urban high school. Nadine and Oscar were both from urban lower-middle-class families. Nadine moved to New York City at age nine, whereas Oscar received his primary and secondary education in prestigious urban schools in Jamaica. He migrated to New York City in 1994 at age 20. Both Nadine and Oscar were mesolectal to acrolectal speakers.

I chose Guyanese and Jamaican students because research has shown that with respect to the Creole continuum, Guyanese and Jamaican Creoles include the most basilectal varieties along with a wide range of mesolectal varieties (Alleyne, 1980; Rickford, 1987; Winford, 1991). Students from Guyana and Jamaica are thus more likely to be basilectal to mesolectal speakers and to exhibit creolized features in their attempts to write standard English. Furthermore, because Guyana and Jamaica have the highest rates of immigration from the English-speaking Caribbean, there is a greater likelihood that instructors will encounter students from these countries in New York City colleges.

DATA COLLECTION

Interviews

I tape-recorded and transcribed several interviews with the participants to document their educational experiences in Guyana and Jamaica as well as in New York City, their views on their own education with respect to language and writing, and their linguistic experiences as new immigrants in New York City schools. The interview questions fell under three categories:

A: Biographical
1. What is your date and place of birth?
2. Where did you grow up? Was it an urban or rural area?
3. Describe your family —for example, number of siblings, occupation of parents.
4. When did you migrate to the United States? Who sponsored you?
5. How old were you when you migrated?

B: Formal education
(in your country)
1. What was the highest level of schooling attained in your country?

2. Did you attend urban or rural schools?
3. Were they traditional/academic or vocational schools?

(in New York City)
4. Did you attend elementary, middle or high school in New York City? If answer is yes, give name and location of school.
5. In what grade were you placed on entering school in New York City?
6. Do you have a regular high school diploma or high school equivalency diploma (GED)? Give year diploma was granted.
7. When did you start attending LIU?

C: Language and writing
(in your country)
1. What would you call your first language or the language spoken in your home?
2. How would you characterize the attitude towards your home language in school? Was it encouraged? Discouraged or stigmatized? Allowed in specific contexts?
3. What are your earliest recollections of reading/writing at home and school? You might discuss how often you read/wrote. What kinds of texts did you read/write? Was there much reading/writing in your home?

(in New York City)
4. How did administrators and teachers respond to your speech and writing when you first entered school in New York City?
5. Were you ever placed in an ESL, remedial, or special education class because of your language? Describe the experience.
6. How did other students react to your speech initially?
7. Did you notice any changes over time in teachers' and students' attitudes towards your speech and writing? Explain.
8. Describe any changes you have noticed in your own speech and writing since migrating to New York City.
9. What kinds of texts did you read/write in high school?
10. How do you feel about your writing at LIU? How has it changed since being in the writing program?
11. Which writing assignments are the most challenging for you? Explain.
12. What kinds of writing do you do best and why?

Corpus of Written Material

I also collected as much of the participants' writing as possible from English 13 through 17. This included drafts of revised essays, in-class essays, research papers, journal writing, free writing, and their midterm and end-of-term portfolios.

The resulting collection of work was arranged in an ordered sequence and thus constituted a representative sample of the participants' writing over two academic years. I separated the data of each participant by course level—English 13, then 14, and so forth. This created an automatic sorting of the writing into various genres, as English 13 and 14 were mostly autobiographical or narrative with some introductory argumentation in English 14, English 16 was mainly expository, and English 17 research. For English 13, 14, and 16, I set aside the midterm and final portfolios for each participant. Portfolios were the primary source of data for my analysis because they provided a representative sample of the participant's writing, both formal and informal. The contents of the portfolio were chosen by the student and typically included one or two revised essays with drafts, an essay written in class, one piece of informal writing (usually a journal entry), and a cover letter/self-assessment in which the student reflected on his/her own writing process and development. For English 17, the research papers were the data for my analysis.

DATA ANALYSIS

Interviews

One of my concerns in transcribing the interviews was the choice of an appropriate orthographic system to reflect accurately the spoken language of the participants. Their speech, as will be seen in the excerpts from the interviews in the following chapters, alternated between Creole English and standard English pronunciations. Sometimes the students used Creole English and standard English pronunciations within the same sentence, as in the following example from Myrna (Creole English pronunciations are underlined):

> Like back '<u>ome</u> they give you a subject, you '<u>ave</u> to write on somet'ing— they just kind <u>o'</u> like look for the answer in the paper, but like over '<u>ere</u> it's more proofreading, like it gotta be more descriptive, more substance, more analysis, more examples.

This mixing of codes might be attributed to the formality of the interview situation combined with my own unique position as both outsider and insider relative to the participants. On the one hand, the participants saw me as a college professor to whom they should show the requisite respect by speaking standard English; on the other hand, they saw me as a Guyanese, a fellow Caribbean with whom they could relax and revert to the vernacular.

Striving for accuracy in the transcriptions was a difficult task. In the case of this study, there was the danger of overmarking Creole English features, thereby giving a false impression of the students' actual speech. Nevertheless, I tried to convey the character and expressiveness of the four. participants by remaining as true to their actual pronunciation as possible.

The following key is an adaptation of Rickford's (1987) phonetic guide to Guyanese Creole English pronunciation along with some of my own observations of the participants' pronunciation. Although the guide is based on Guyanese Creole English, the pronunciation patterns are similar enough to Jamaican Creole English, at least in regard to the sound-spelling correspondences listed, such that they can be applied to all of the participants.

Key to Pronunciation

Creole English   Standard American English
Initial consonants
[t]—ting   [th]—thing
[d]—dat   [dh]—that
[ky]—kyañ   [k]—can't
[ ]—'ome   [h]—home

Final consonants
[n']—nuttin'   [ng]—nothing
[n']—don'*   [n't]—don't
[s]—jus'*   [st]—just

*The word-final consonant pronunciations are only some possibilities among many.

Vowels
[i]—di   [e]—the
[e]—tek   [a]—take
[uh]—yuh   [oo]—you
[a]—bady   [o]—body
final [a]—matta   final [er]—matter

The analysis of the interviews was a two-fold process. First, I selected, transcribed, and discussed excerpts from each of the participant's responses that directly addressed four broad themes:

1. The participant's early literacy practices at home and school: for example,

    You know we started out with basic writin' like small topics . . . you know the name of the school. I remember like composition stuff . . . like it was based on the school and we had to tell the teacher about that school . . . the name of the principals and all o' dat. (Oscar)

2. The attitudes towards the vernacular in the participant's home country and in New York City: for example,

    Sometimes my mother doesn't wanna hear it [Creole] but she speaks like that, too. (Nadine)

3. The participant's views of his/her own spoken language: for example,

    Yep, that's [Jamaican Creole] just about most of what I speak every day because most of the time I'm around Jamaicans. (Oscar)

4. The participant's reflections on his/her college writing: for example,

    You know 'the girls walk' and 'a girl walks' . . . yeah, I got that together now. . . . I think I got better—much, much better. (Nadine)

Second, I compared the excerpts to determine similarities and differences across the participants with respect to each of the four themes. These excerpts were also used as a basis to compare whether the participants' views of their spoken and written language reflected their actual speech and writing.

Corpus of Written Material

I examined the writing of the participants in order to characterize what I referred to earlier as their academic interlanguage, that is, the written language that emerged when they negotiated their own Creole English with standard English. I also compared the writings across the participants, documenting striking similarities or differences in their features and describing their approximations of standard English relative to each other. Because the participants have all had different linguistic experiences both at home and at school (in New York City and in their home countries), I felt it was important to do a close analysis of their writing to show how those experiences were reflected therein.

To answer my second research question, the corpus was analyzed on two levels: first, for certain discourse features of essayist literacy and second, for morphosyntactic features. I used oral/written language features as described by Halliday (1989) and Chafe and Danielewicz (1987) as a heuristic tool.

As previously mentioned, Halliday delineates the following characteristics of written essayist language (all examples are taken from the participants' writing):

1. Greater verbal explicitness:

   According to Fish, the "you" who does the interpretive work that puts poems, lists and assignments into the world is a communal you. In other words, we create assignments through strategies that are not our own because they are "always shared and public."

   The second sentence begins with the prepositional phrase [i]n other words, which signals that the previous sentence will be further explained. [I]nterpretive work in sentence one is simplified to strategies in sentence two and communal is explained as shared and public.

2. Strong tendency to encode language in nominal form:

   Reading and writing plays important roles in our everyday lives.

   The example above shows the nominalization of the verbs read and write.

3. Frequent use of hypotaxis:

   The second most difficult paper was the in-class essay which I tried keeping the topic in focus, in order to produce a good essay.

   The sentence above includes a relative clause beginning with <u>which</u> and a subordinate clause beginning with <u>in order to</u>.

4. High ratio of lexical density. Lexical density is calculated by the number of lexical items (content words) versus the number of grammatical items (function words) relative to the total running words. Grammatical items are those that function in closed systems in the language such as determiners (including articles), pronouns, most prepositions, conjunctions, and auxiliary verbs. Lexical items are an open class in the language and include nouns, lexical verbs, adjectives, adverbs, and some prepositions. The following example illustrates a sentence with a high ratio of lexical density ("L" indicates lexical items; "G" indicates grammatical items):

   Freire and Fish express their views under the concepts of "banking" and communal category of thought respectively.

   The sentence has 17 running words.
   10 lexical items—Freire, Fish, express, views, concept, banking, communal, category, thought, respectively.
   7 grammatical items—and, their, under, the, of, and, of.
   Ratio of lexical density: L: 10; G: 7 (59%)
   Type/token ratio: 15/17 or .88

The statistics above suggest that when there is a high ratio of lexical density and a high type/token ratio, the language has a more written feel. A high type/token ratio suggests less repetition of words.

I did a qualitative analysis of the data with respect to the first three characteristics and described a lesser or greater degree of verbal explicitness as corresponding to nonessayist oral or essayist written language respectively. In addition, writing that contained greater use of action verbs was considered to exhibit features of oral language whereas greater use of passive verbs was considered more typical of written language.

In terms of lexical density, I did a quantitative analysis on each participant's research paper. Given that the research paper was the most formal academic writing done by the participants, it was more likely to reveal a high ratio of lexical density. The research paper from each participant was analyzed in detail, calculating the ratio of lexical density for the first 400 running words (two sets of 200 words each). This allowed a more precise comparison across the four participants. I then calculated the type/token ratio for the same 400 words to get a sense of the range of items. The participants' research papers are discussed along a continuum ranging from more oral to more written language, as lexical density and type/token ratios are lower or higher respectively.

Morphosyntactic Analysis

A pilot study of one of the participants, Charles, revealed that language transfer and overgeneralization of standard English rules were the two most common processes involved on the syntactic level when the Creole English speaker attempts to write in standard English. Thus, a general qualitative analysis was done on each participant's writing focusing on language transfer and overgeneralization of standard English rules with respect to six morphosyntactic features. Then, a quantitative analysis was done on the first 400 words of each participant's research paper in regard to the same features to gain a more accurate comparison across the participants. I counted only actual occurrences of errors relative to possible occurrences. Features were based on Roberts' (1988) research. Roberts' features were chosen precisely because they represent one of the most palpable differences between Creole English and standard English—the absence/presence of inflections. The use of inflections is not only a prominent feature of standard English but has also become an indicator of "literateness" in the Western linguistic tradition—a phenomenon that ought to be reexamined. Most students, especially those who speak noninflected languages such as Creole English, grapple constantly with inflections in essayist writing, often resulting in some combination of language transfer and overgeneralization of standard English rules. Because of the differences between Creole English and standard English, I hypothesized that verb inflections would be particularly challenging for the participants in this study.

The following features were analyzed. All examples of the participants' writing below and in each of the following narratives were left intact—errors in syntax, spelling, and pronunciation were not corrected. Asterisks indicate what would be considered errors in standard English.

1. Verb-related features.
   (a) Zero copula:
      Those boys * tough.

(b) Zero inflection for subject/verb agreement:
When someone read* my work, they should feel the need to go on until the end.
(c) Zero inflection for tense (tense is indicated by the context):
I didn't think that it look* provocative. (Didn't sets up the past tense context).
(d) Zero inflection for verb participles:
I was a little disappointed to what I had encounter*.
(e) Overgeneralization of standard English verb inflection for third person singular and past tense:
The essays in the class anthology says* a lot about identity.
I didn't knew* the answer.

2. Zero marking for plurals, especially after number words or determiners that modify a plural noun. Plural -s is seen as redundant:
Judith Cofer and Virginia Woolf are writer* of two book* of memoirs.

3. Zero marking for possession. Possession is shown by the juxtaposition of possessor and possessed, as opposed to the standard English genitive marker 's:
Paul* problem get bigger went he started drinking.

4. Phonological influence on spelling:
Writing journal entry as* helped me to understand the book much better.

5. Sentence focus:
The thing about my sex life, it was great taking good care and protection of myself.

6. Creole English use of standard English grammatical words.
Students does go on like that = (Students go on like that).

5

Charles Benjamin

I get a high school diploma, but I don' feel like I earn it honestly, 'cause I really didn't get nuttin' from school.

Charles Benjamin was born on December 3, 1971, in a village called Rosehall in Berbice, Guyana. The fifth of six children, Charles was raised with his two brothers and three sisters in a low-income family that he describes as close-knit and very religious. His father was a carpenter, and his mother worked as a maid in the homes of middle-income residents in their village.

Charles was somewhat shy, but could be very candid once he became comfortable with his interviewer. He was a tall young man of medium build with a deep voice and a distinctly rural Guyanese accent. Having grown up in a typical rural village in Guyana with many of its residents being sugar cane cutters or small-scale tradespeople, Charles acquired the basilectal speech of what Rickford (1987) calls "the estate class" (named after the laborers who worked on the sugar estates). His pronunciation and syntax were largely basilectal, with some shifting toward the mesolect whenever we conducted tape-recorded interviews.

EARLY LANGUAGE AND SCHOOLING EXPERIENCES

Charles referred to his home language as *Creolese*, a term used by many Guyanese to refer to the vernacular, adding that "everybady from di village does talk Creolese." He was very aware of what he called his "strong accent," in particular, when contrasted with his parents who he felt have "no type of accent at all." I asked him to elaborate on the difference between his and his parents' speech:

> Well, I don' know...is just different with me...'cause sometimes you know when I speak and dey speak, I does t'ink...but I don' sound nuttin' like dem...sometimes I get so frustrated...so I jus' leave it like dat.

Charles did not recall his vernacular being stigmatized at home or in school. However, when he visited a larger town in Berbice called New Amsterdam or went to Georgetown, the capital city, he was very conscious of his speech. Many Georgetown residents referred to him as "country man" based on his rural speech and demeanor. It was not surprising that he decided not to visit Georgetown very often.

Charles did very little reading or writing at home. He noted that reading at home was mostly confined to the Bible: "My mother, she just get everybady to the Bible stuff." His early schooling was at Rosehall Scots Primary School, which he attended until age 11. Then, because of his low marks on the Common Entrance Examination (a national entrance exam used as the main criterion for placing students into high school), he attended a vocational school called Port Morant Community High School. Both schools were located in rural Berbice; thus, Charles was immersed in basilectal speech outside the classroom. Community high schools were nontraditional, vocational schools for students whose scores on the Common Entrance Exam were not sufficiently high to be placed into a traditional academic high school. The curriculum, facilities, and staffing at such schools suffered from a serious lack of resources in comparison to traditional high schools, and there was often a high dropout rate. Furthermore, Charles went to high school in the 1980s when Guyana was in the midst of an economic crisis, and so many schools suffered from understaffing, limited facilities, and equipment. Not surprisingly, schools in the rural areas, which were usually given low priority, were most harshly affected. Charles described the conditions in his community high school:

> Di school was overcrowded. Di majority o' di class couldn't keep inside....Dey had to keep outside on di grass....Nobady was payin' attention. Dey was not a lot o' chalkboard and books and dose t'ings.

In fact, Charles only went to school one day a week. He found the conditions in school so deplorable that they were not conducive to learning. When asked what he did for the rest of the week, he responded, "I use to go to a private school. Mi gra'mudda cousin, she use to keep a private school, so mos' o' di time we use to go dere to do English, like tutorin'."

Charles did not do much reading or writing in school or even prescriptive grammar exercises, which was typically done in many English classes in primary school in Guyana. He admitted that English was not one of his favorite subjects, but he "got by." His favorite subject was math. He pointed out that his tutoring only lasted for four or five months, so it was very little help in terms of developing verbal or mathematical literacies.

Obviously disillusioned by his school experiences in Guyana, Charles recalled that many of his peers dropped out of school, choosing cane-cutting as a more lucrative lifestyle. Reflecting on growing up in Guyana during harsh economic times, he lamented, "It was 'ard, real 'ard... honestly, I really don' fin' Guyana 'ave nuttin' fo' me...nuttin' really goin' on over dere. Everybady wanna come up 'ere" [meaning the United States].

MIGRATION AND SCHOOLING IN NEW YORK CITY

In May 1986, Charles migrated to New York City. His entire family was sponsored by his uncle although Charles came to New York City first by himself. His family later migrated in stages (a process known as *staggered migration*). Charles explained:

> My uncle sponsored us. He sponsored di whole family, but it jus' happen dat...I don' know how it happen, but my paper get t'rough before anybady else, so it was me first, den mi fadda, den mi mudda, den all di rest come.

It took approximately two years before Charles' parents and siblings finally migrated and joined him. In the meantime, he was living with his uncle. Once settled in New York City, his mother found a job as a nurse's aide and his father began working as a handyman. The family eventually bought a house, and they have all been living together since then.

Like many Guyanese who left their country in the mid 1980s, Charles felt more relieved to have left home than excited about being in New York City. In September 1986, he enrolled in Boys and Girls High School in Bedford-Stuyvesant, Brooklyn, and was placed in the ninth grade. Boys and Girls turned out to be an unpleasant experience both academically and socially.

Having been so poorly schooled in Guyana, Charles found it difficult to cope with his academic subjects. He confessed:

> It was difficult, because how yuh use to do certain tings back 'ome...you kyañ [can't] do it over 'ere...like di mat' and di 'istory...'cause certain way yuh know to do di mat', is very different over 'ere...I had to get a tutor for dat till I really get it down dey way.

When asked if he had difficulty with English, he replied:

> No, 'cause I really never use to 'ave a problem wit' English. Dey neva really use to do a lot o' writin' in 'igh school...jus' read a passage and fill in di blank...not much essay writin'....Mos' o' di work we did in class. It wasn' a lot o' writin'.

Charles' comments were symptomatic of his literacy issues. He had "no problem" with writing because he had virtually no practice with the process. Ironically, Charles claimed that math and English were his two best subjects in high school and noted, "other subjects, I wasn' graspin'."

Compounding his academic dilemma was what Charles characterized as a "hostile" environment at Boys and Girls vis-à-vis Caribbean students. He offered a graphic description of a typical day at Boys and Girls:

> A typical day at Boys and Girls is like goin' to the fish market and you and t'ree odda people fightin' fuh di same fish....Sometimes... some days it was so intense, yuh jus' get so frustrated...yuh wan' tek out yuh anga on somet'ing, but yuh don't, yuh jus' calm down and jus' go t'rough it.

I asked Charles what exactly made him so angry—was it the teachers or the students? He explained that it was mostly the students:

> When I came over 'ere, it was kinda hard...was kinda hostile t'ing for Caribbean students....Now you might be the only Caribbean student sittin' among American students, and you know how dey stay [are]...

dey come and say...oh, you comin' fuh tek 'way we jobs...dis and da....It was kinda hard.

Charles admitted that many times he thought of "getting even" with the American students, but his favorite teacher, a Jamaican man, told him, "it don' wort' it, 'cause dat's di way dey is." So Charles ignored the taunts and managed to get through high school.

In 1992, he graduated from Boys and Girls. Reflecting on his high school experience, he lamented,

> I get a high school diploma, but I don' feel like I earn it honestly, 'cause I really didn' get nuttin' from school....Dat's why I gotta do everyt'ing...so I really look forward to gettin' a college degree.

Still, in the year-and-a-half between high school and college, Charles confessed that he did nothing to prepare himself academically for college. As he put it, "when I stop high school, I jus' stop everyt'ing in general." He felt that it might have been a phase he was going through:

> I was going t'rough a phase between high school and college. I was like indecisive—whether I must go to college or go and tek up a trade or somet'ing...so I was kinda going t'rough a phase right dere...so I drop everyt'ing and jus' clear my mind up. When I try to do it [school work] now, it's kinda difficult. I don' know why.

WRITING AT LIU

In Fall 1993, Charles began classes at LIU, intending to major in nursing. It should come as no surprise that he was placed into English 13. Given his minimal reading and writing skills, he needed to be in an intensive reading and writing program. One of the most striking features of Charles' writing was his unfamiliarity with standard English grammar rules and writing conventions. Having had very little practice with writing or exposure to the print code, he relied almost exclusively on his speech for syntax and spelling. As a result, there was a marked orality in his writing and inconsistency in his application of syntactic rules. In formal writing assignments where Charles was expected to adhere to standard written English conventions, his writing appeared inconsistent and was more prone to error in form. However, in assignments where he was able to draw on oral language, his writing appeared to be more effective, as is shown on the following page.

DISCOURSE ANALYSIS

Informal Writing

In English 14 Charles wrote a dialogue in which he was able to render the orality of casual conversation effectively in writing. Just as Halliday (1989) notes that personal letters can be viewed as oral texts in writing, so dialogues can be viewed in a similar way. One difference between the two is that dialogues may involve more than two persons and include a dramatic element. Also, the text in a dialogue alternates between the written language of contextual cues and the oral language of participants. The dialogue written by Charles involved a young man named Roger and his parents and focused on Roger's relationship with a young woman with whom he bore a child. The following is an excerpt from the dialogue:

One day while sitting in the living room the phone ring, it a girl for Roger.

```
        Mother:  Roger, there is a girl on the phone.
        Roger:   Who is it?
        Mother:  Some girl say her name is gina and stop hiding form [from]
                 her.
 5      Popa:    Isn't that the girl I see you with the night in front the store?
        Roger:   Yes.
        Popa:    That was fast, it donot take you long to do something then
                 start hiding right.
10      Mother:  Would both of you shut up you all are acting like babies.
        Popa:    Woman, you dose [does] not like the idea that your son is talk-
                 ing to a young lady.
        Mother:  Talking is not the problem, but when you are doing something
                 else, that a hole big deal.
15      Popa:    Then what is the problem and please donot say nothing.
        Mother:  Why don't you ask your son since you see the girl and I didn't.
        Popa:    I thought you brougth the girls to see your mother boy.
        Roger:   No
20      Popa:    Why didn't you bring the girl to see your mother?
        Roger:   You know how mother act when she see I bring some body
                 new in the house.
        Popa:    He is right, dear, you all ways act like how long is this one is
                 going to last for.
25      Mother:  Oh, that the way you all feel. ok, just remember that I was a
                 young lady once and that is wrong, what your son's doing.
        Popa:    What is that?
        Mother:  Use young lady like they are a pecace [piece] of tools.
```

Although standard English words are used in constructing the dialogue, there is a decidedly Creole "feel" to the text. Since Charles described the participants in the dialogue as people from "the islands," the use of Creole English was quite appropriate. Charles vividly rendered the spontaneity of speech on the page, leaving meanings to be inferred from context. For example, in lines 8-9, "[t]hat was fast, it donot take you long to do something then start hiding," we can surmise that <u>that</u> refers to the developing relationship between Roger and the young woman; <u>something</u> implies a possible intimate encounter between the two. When Roger's father suggests that Roger's mother does not like her son "talking to a young lady" (line 12), <u>talking</u> is used in the Creole English sense of getting to know someone with the intention of dating and possibly becoming sexually involved with that person.

Charles incorporated features typical of casual, spoken language into the dialogue, for example, the phrase "shut up" (line 10) or the mid-sentence embedded question, "like how long is this one is going to last for" (line 23-24). He was able to capture the emotion involved in the conversation by utilizing the features of oral communication effectively. Despite the spelling errors, the reader is drawn into an interesting exchange. (See Appendix B for the full text of the dialogue.)

Formal Writing

In English 13, Charles wrote an essay in response to Piri Thomas' memoir *Down These Mean Streets*, which describes his (Thomas') experience as a Puerto Rican immigrant in New York City. Charles compared his experience as a Guyanese immigrant to Thomas' immigrant experience. Following is an excerpt from a draft of his essay.

> My first experience was at school it was rough way to start school for a stranger to this country. The reason is a youth from the carribbean never has it easy because you are never welcome or an outcast to everyone and everything. They feel that you come here to take
> 5 something away from them meaning the 'bullies' in school. They would start calling you names like, 'hey banana boat boy why did you come here why don't you go back where you came from' so if the name calling does not work they tend to find something else to do with you. For example, like one day while walking in the park a group of boys
> 10 come up to me and said where did you come from and my answer was Guyana with that answer they starteed a bunch of nonsense that could make some one do something to them which you might not be cut out to do.

>   With all this happening I felt that my dad or the people that I hung out
> 15   with did not prepare for this. So I started to get mad and acting foolish
>   also rebeling against everything that my parents standards were for or
>   anyone around me. I thought that everything was happening for a
>   reason but when I got to find out this was a bigamist and where
>   everyone is playing a bully to those that are a stranger to the place. I
> 20   thought that it would get much better not since i met some of my
>   friends from back home ane we come up with an idea of starting
>   a disc-jacket system. But I was wrong. The first day I went to go and did
>   it and was robbed by two guys about the same age as myself. They took
>   all my gold, money and tore up my clothes. To make matters worst it
> 25   was freezing that night which I did not wear a coat.

The narrative sustains a central idea, that is, the problems Charles encountered as a new immigrant. The writing shows what Halliday (1989) describes as features of oral language, especially a high frequency of action verbs, for example, "they would start calling" (lines 5-6), "one day while walking" (line 9), "a group of boys came up to me" (lines 9-10), "they started" (line 11), "with all this happening I felt" (line 14), "I started to get mad and acting foolish" (line 15). In addition, the narrative includes a running commentary of Charles' emotional response to events. He created an oral, interactive text by constantly telling how he felt, thought, acted, and was affected by events. This is an example of Chafe and Danielewicz' (1987) notion of "involvement of self" in oral discourse. Charles also used terms that appear vague to the reader, perhaps with the presumption that the reader knew what he meant, for example, "a bunch of nonsense that could make some one do something" (lines 11-12). It is unclear what "nonsense" or "something" means. He appeared to be representing a shared context rather than sharing a context with the reader. The lack of verbal explicitness based on a presumption of shared understanding is a common feature of oral discourse (Ong, 1982).

Charles also had a tendency to string ideas together in the same sentence, creating run-on sentences and leaving the reader at a loss for his intended meaning, for example, "So I started to get mad and acting foolish also rebeling against everything that my parents standards were for or anyone around me" (lines 15-17). It is unclear whether "anyone around me" means Charles' rebelling against anyone who happened to be close to him, like his parents, or anyone who had similar standards to his parents. Later, in line 18, the word "bigamist" leaves the reader somewhat puzzled. (In the context, I can only conjecture that Charles might have meant "big mess".) In line 20, the sentence is derailed with the use of "not." The negative marker does not fit the meaning of the sentence.

Charles demonstrated his inexperience with essayist writing by his inconsistent application of rules of punctuation and other conventions of the genre. "Guyana" (line 11) is capitalized, "carribbean" (line 2) is not; direct speech in lines 6-7 is put in quotation marks, whereas quotation marks are omitted in line 10. "i" is written in lower case in line 20, but capitalized elsewhere. Occasionally, Charles correctly applied the rules of standard written English. In lines 4-5, he showed an awareness of the rule that requires pronouns to have corresponding referents: <u>They</u> and <u>them</u> are thus explained by the cataphoric reference "the bullies in school." In lines 9-11 he offered an example to explain <u>something else</u>: "For example like one day while walking in the park a group of boys came up to me and said where did you come from . . . they started a bunch of nonsense."

As writing assignments became less autobiographical and more analytical, Charles grappled with the greater demand on his writing skills. In English 14, he was asked to write an essay in response to Gloria Naylor's *Women of Brewster Place*, a novel in part about one woman's dream to move her community beyond their impoverished circumstances as symbolized by a brick wall. The assignment required students to discuss the significance of the wall. The following is an excerpt from Charles' first draft of the assignment:

>   The meaning of a real or a symbolic wall in the Women of Brewster Place was that the wall was very much real because it was keeping the people who was living in brewster place down. The reason for that is to them from seeing what they was missing on the other side. This wall
> 5 was to make them lost all hope and a sense of direction in which they had. So they would think that this is the last stop for them. . . .
>
>   On the other hand a symbolic wall is something that put up by a person that wanted to remember peoples by so they would form a committe that would put formous [famous] people face and name and what they
> 10 have been down [doing] for their envoirment or country. But the wall on Brewster place was nothing like that it was keeping people like Mattie and the other that was living under her down.

The excerpt above shows Charles' trying to make sense not only of the story but of the assignment. He begins by trying to define the key terms in the assignment—"real or symbolic wall." In so doing, the writing appears to be circular at times, for example, in lines 1-2 when he says the meaning of a real or symbolic wall "was that the wall was very much real," the repetition of "real" indicates difficulty with explication. His explanation of a "symbolic wall" reflects a curious misreading of the text. Although he recognized that the wall in Brewster Place was not like a symbolic wall where names of famous people are placed, he failed to see that it was not real at all. As an inexperienced reader, Charles was unable to distinguish between the literal and the metaphorical, which affected his understanding of and response to writing assignments. He never revised the draft of this essay.

Charles did not pass English 14. At the time he took the course, the portfolio system of evaluation had not yet been institutionalized; thus, passing the course was based on an exit exam, which he failed. The writing program offered a special summer writing workshop for those students who failed the exit exam. Charles took and successfully completed the workshop and was allowed to register for English 16.

In-Class Writing

In English 16, he continued to grapple with challenging writing assignments. In-class writing was particularly difficult, given the limited amount of time. For Charles, as writing assignments demanded more abstraction, his discourse became, paradoxically, more concrete. As mentioned earlier, Chafe and Danielewicz (1987) contend that concrete referents are more typical of oral language. In an essay in response to Harriet Jacobs' *Incidents in the Life of a Slave Girl*, he wrote:

> She [Jacobs] was always treated like a slave, in order sense she was like a on and off switch. This mean when the order [other] slave like she was around she was one of them, when they not around she was some what equal to the master.

Note that Charles used a concrete referent, "on and off switch" to characterize Jacobs. Relying primarily on an oral base, which tends to frame issues close to the human life world (Ong, 1982), Charles tried to describe Jacobs in terms most familiar to him. He compared Jacobs' alternating between acting like a slave and being equal to the master to a switch being turned on and off. Despite the graphic explanation, Charles' instructor noted that the writing was not clear. Still, this might have been his best attempt at making sense of the text.

Research Paper

Charles' unfamiliarity with essayist writing conventions made research a formidable challenge. It should be noted that he was in my English 17X class—a class for non-native speakers of English. Charles struggled with many of the same issues as regular ESL students. In fact, he had more difficulty with writing than the majority of his classmates. Whereas most ESL students had strong first language literacies, Charles was an inexperienced reader and writer in English, which is officially his first language.

The first research project required students to interview two non-native speakers of English outside of their own ethnic group, with a view to examining the role of language in their immigrant experiences. Charles successfully interviewed two Brooklyn-based cab drivers—one Mexican and the other Haitian—but he was unable to incorporate the interviews into his paper effectively. In the final draft of his paper, the introduction and the conclusion each consisted of one sentence. The introduction read as follows: "The role of language in immigration seen thought [through] of my two interviewee Johnny and Martinez." Having had no experience with research and having read so little, Charles had no frame of reference for developing an introduction. His conclusion was as follows: "In my final thoughts; As they say a hard head make a soft butt, which I think these two men was." In the absence of analysis, Charles concluded with a popular Guyanese proverb. He seemed unable to extract and discuss issues emanating from the interviews. Instead, he relied on a common practice in oral cultures—using a proverb to conclude a story.

Charles' final research paper discussed the recent wave of Guyanese immigrants to the United States, including their reasons for migrating and their settlement patterns. In this paper, he made an effort to write a more explicit introduction as seen below:

> This a study of Guyanese immigrate from the late 70's to the late 80's. In this study I would expose why there were a large shift of Guyanese in those period. Also look at why they came and how they are dealing with the present time.

Despite the grammatical errors (<u>immigrate</u> should be <u>immigrants</u> and <u>were</u> should be <u>was</u>), the reader is given a sense of what the paper is about. However, Charles had difficulty sustaining clarity in the rest of the paper. Following is an excerpt of the final draft:

> Between the late 1970 and the early 1980 Guyana the leading countries that were supplying the United State with legal immigrant. The reason why alot people were left the country was that Guyana was about to faced a change in their political system and the economic system would

5   also face problem too. And alot of people knew what when on the last
    time that this person while he was in office. It was 1981 or 1982 I reality
    couldn't remember which it was, but it was around election time when
    a person called Forbes Benhan was elected to the office. This president
    was a night-mare for alot of poor mority people that were living there,
10 because his theory was not for them.
    With all of this going the immigrant office in Guyana continue to
    accept people application for a vista to leave. This cause the shift in
    Guyana history of immigrant to ever leave the country like that and
    rank Guyana in the top country in which people was migrate like that.
15 As you can see Guyana was identy by his economic problem that cause
    his people to leave like that. This was just a piece of the pie between
    those year, because things would never get better in term of economic
    change . . .

    As the year's began to go up thing started to look dim for Guyana. The
20 United State began to receive more and more people from Guyana. The
    particular nationality composition of these flow is expected to continue
    in coming despite in the 1980 from Guyana. The mandate calling for
    the greater diversification the nationally mix and carries significant
    implication for accelerating the of change in New York ethic make-up.

25 Although the rank of Guyanese people were not consist there were still
    a large number of them that were making a great impact and the rest of
    that was facing a hard time in Guyana. Between 1988 and 1989 the
    number of legal immigrant that was coming from and who was
    selected for residence in New York City was more than forty thousand
30 each year. This statistics was down by Nadia Youssef who wrote a book
    call, "The Demographic of Immigrant," that deal with the number of
    immigrant that come's in to American from the caribbean. As a
    portion of the nation wide number legally admitted into the United
    State between 88 and 89, 74% of them is Guyanese.

The lexical density of the first 200 words above (ending in line 17) is L: 69; G: 131, compared to the next 200 words (ending in line 34) which is L: 80; G: 120. The higher ratio of lexical density in paragraphs three and four gives them a more written feel. The language in this section, though, seems at odds with the rest of Charles' writing, suggesting that it might have been plagiarized. Words and phrases such as "mandate" (line 22), "greater diversification" (line 23), and "significant implication" (line 23-24) appear to be taken from secondary sources. Unfortunately, there is no documentation of such sources.

Whenever there was a higher ratio of lexical density, the writing seemed to be plagiarized. Still, taking plagiarism into account, the total lexical density in 400 words of Charles' research paper was L: 149; G: 251 (37%). This is a rather low ratio of lexical density for a research paper (the most formal kind of academic writing). Furthermore, the type/token ratio for the same 400 words was 177/400 or .44, suggesting a narrow range in his use of words or, put another way, many repeated items.

In regard to verbal explicitness, many sentences in this research paper were poorly structured and included several morphosyntactic errors, resulting in a loss of intended meaning. For example in lines 5-6, "[a]nd alot of people knew what when on the last time that this person while he was in office," the reader is not told what went on. The sentence also goes syntactically awry after "person," as there is no verb. In line 10, Charles wrote that the president's "theory" was not for the people; yet, there is no explanation of the theory. In any case, the word "policy" might have been more appropriate here than "theory." Later, we are left to infer the meanings of "like that" in lines 13-14, and lines 21-22 lose their meaning after "expected to continue in coming." These are examples of what Coleman (1995) calls *consolidation of propositions*, a phenomenon that Shaughnessy (1977) attributes to oral interference. Consolidation of propositions is the merging of two or more incomplete propositions in one sentence. In line 22, the reader expects a noun after the word "coming" but instead Charles uses the word "despite" to begin a new proposition which is also incomplete:

1. The particular nationality composition of these flow is expected to continue in coming . . . ?
2. . . . despite in the 1980 from Guyana.

I wondered if Charles might have been making assumptions of shared knowledge, as his research paper was on Guyanese immigration and he was aware that the instructor was Guyanese. The rest of the paper had many more syntactically incorrect sentences, making Charles' ideas very difficult to understand.

I also analyzed the first 400 words of Charles' research paper for selected morphosyntactic features mentioned in the methodology. The results are summarized in Table 2.

Table 2 reveals that Charles shows a strong propensity for error in at least three areas: inflections for third person singular (100% error), generic count nouns (75%) and possessives (100%). We see that even in the final draft of a research paper (which presupposes that a fair amount of editing has been done), Charles' writing revealed a high percentage of error in three major categories.

Table 2. Morphosyntactic Features. Total Number of Morphosyntactic Errors in 400 Words of Charles' Research Paper.

	Actual Occurrences	Possible Occurrences
Verb-Related Features		
Zero copula	2	25
Zero inflection for:		
third person singular	2	2
past tense	5	36
verb particles	3	13
Plurals		
Zero inflection for:		
noun with plural determiner	2	5
generic count nouns	9	12
Possessives		
Zero inflection on possessor:	1	1
Total:	24	94

A general qualitative analysis of Charles' writing from English 100 to 300 revealed morphosyntactic errors in all the areas investigated.

Verb-related Features: Zero Copula

The following examples were taken from the dialogue mentioned earlier about a conversation between a young man named Roger and his parents.

Mother: Oh that* the way you feel . . .
Roger: How can you do something like that to me without telling me?
Mother: Just like how you father meet her and I didn't, that* how.

In the example above, it is unclear whether Charles was following the Creole English rule for zero copula in phrases that function as predicative complements or simply writing sentences the way he hears them or thinks they would be said in a real conversation. In any case, the absence of copula in this context is appropriate because it reflects accurately the language of a Creole English dialogue.

In journal entries he wrote:

1. Went [when] you turn on the TV, the evening new, it* not like you are going to see anything different.
2. That* the way I feel went I see these rose grow and burst out.
3. The only thing I can think about is the land, that* the only place I can really put myself.

Other Verb-Related Features

Charles' writing showed errors in past tense, third person singular subject-verb concord, and compound verb phrases including passive structures. There appeared to be no pattern to the syntactic environment in which errors occurred. In some instances, inflections were missing in one part of a sentence but correctly used in another part, as in the following examples:

1. Things were different from the place where he come* from to the new place where he is presently living because it was not what he had hope* for.
2. Paul was a person who think* no one can understand what he was going through in his life.
3. This was eye opener for me because if I had listen* to my parents I would not have gotten myself in this problem.

In other instances there were several errors in the same sentence:

1. He think* that was right so went his friend try* to help him he always say* that in his life, that if he have* a problem he would go to church and pray.
2. That was a big talk went all was finish* in this situation I become* an uncomfortable person breaking on everyone that pass* my way.
3. I choose this story because Piri Thomas have* a great insight on certain things that is* happening to many people who come from different place.
4. This conflict would have never resolve*. But when he have* found out was a whole new game.

Zero Inflection for Possessives

1. Paul* problem get bigger went he started drinking.
2. In many people* eyes he was their God.
3. The immigrant office in Guyana continue to accept people* application for a vista to leave.

Plurals

Zero inflection after determiners that modify a plural noun or after generic count nouns:

1. His father had to work two or three job* just to provide a good home for him.
2. Martinez has faced a lot of problem* during his stay in America.
3. After a couple of week* meeting new people and hear problems . . .
4. Everybody in the world today have problem*.
5. There was also these run down building* which they can fix up and keep all these people from troubling the citizen*.

Sentence Structure

Evidence of front focusing was found:

1. Okay, just remember I was a young lady once and that is wrong, what your son's doing.
2. The thing about my sex life, it was great taking good care and protection of myself.

Phonological Influence on Spelling

The preponderance of spelling errors in Charles' writing went beyond mere phonological influence. They appeared to be of two types:

1. Phonologically influenced

    Charles spells the word as he pronounces it. Target words are in brackets. In Guyanese Creole, [du] is pronounced as [ju]; hence, the phonetic spellings below in (a) and (b).

(a) inter juice   [introduce]
(b) jury   [during]
(c) a pair   [appear]
(d) an order   [another]
(e) pregnent   [pregnant]
(f) accupide   [occupied]

2. Confusion with standard English spelling

(a) went   [when]
(b) uppertion   [operation]
(c) opportious   [opportunity]
(d) mority   [minority]
(e) alaway   [always]

Often, Charles appears to have a sense of the letters in the target word but confuses the order, possibly suggesting a dyslexic condition:

(a) dose   [does]
(b) ture   [true]
(c) dein   [deny]
(d) perthy   [pretty]
(e) augrement   [argument]
(f) edcaution   [education]
(g) resonpable   [responsible]
(h) bearst cancre   [breast cancer]

Creole English Use of Standard English Grammatical Words

As noted by Roberts (1988), the Creole English use of <u>does</u> signals habitual action as opposed to emphasis in standard English. Charles used <u>does</u> with the Creole English meaning in the following examples:

1. He dose not hear, so went the girl reach here I would let she do anything to him.
   In the sentence above, <u>hear</u> carries the Creole English meaning of "listen and take the advice of someone (usually older)." Note also the Creole English use of <u>she</u> as object pronoun. The sentence might be interpreted thus: "He doesn't usually take my advice so when the girl arrives, I will let her do anything to him." There is an unstated message in the sentence which is that the "he" in

question, by habitually ignoring the advice of an elder, ends up offending the girl. Thus, the elder will allow the girl to retaliate in any way she chooses.
2. I never know that students <u>dose</u> go on like that.
The sentence means, "I never knew that students normally behave like that."

Coelho (1991) notes that in Caribbean Creole English a <u>next</u> means <u>another</u> as in the following sentence written by Charles:

1. I know that he did not get a next girl with a kid.

FINAL REFLECTIONS

In the end, Charles did not pass English 17X. After four semesters in the writing program, he was still unable to demonstrate an acceptable level of writing proficiency to be passed on to sophomore literature. Like any inexperienced reader and writer, he needed more time to develop his skills. Reflecting on his writing, Charles expressed regret at not having taken the advice of his English 13 instructor. He lamented, "Di firs' t'ing he [the instructor] tol' me say I gotta get a tutor, I brush it off. . . . I never really tek him on. . . . I wasn' into it." Charles said he wished he had spent more time on his writing. After English 17X, I did not see Charles for two semesters and was afraid he had dropped out.

Just at the point where any hope of hearing from Charles seemed a remote possibility, he reappeared. I found out through a colleague in the English department that Charles had returned to college and had registered once again to take English 17 in the fall 1996 semester. I caught up with him during the third week of the semester and we talked about his absence from school and his plans for the future.

In the two semesters that Charles was out of school, he became a father, changed jobs (from a hospital porter to a drugstore manager), and decided to switch his major from nursing to business administration. He felt that his new job as a manager of a Rite Aid pharmacy in Brooklyn inspired him to change his major. As he put it, "When I start workin' at Rite Aid, I jus' get dis business feel like. I'm relatin' to the business more than like the medical field, so I jus' decide to change it." When Charles told me he worked long hours, I expressed some concern about how he managed to balance his working hours with study time. He explained his time management as follows:

> Basically, I work from four to eight (in the evening). After work, I go home, tek a little snack and get a coupla hours sleep. Then I get up like when the house quiet, then I could do most o' my studyin', most o' my readin', like from twelve midnight to t'ree in the mornin'.

Charles confessed that his father was still skeptical about his return to school. As he put it, "My father cry [worries] every day—well how long it gon tek you before you come out again?," to which Charles replied, "Watch and see, I'm not gonna come out." Whether Charles would drop out again or stay in school remains to be seen. In order to return to classes, he had to sign a promissory note to the dean stating that he would maintain at least a "B" average in his courses. I hope he will be able to keep his promise.

6

Myrna George

> Sometimes when I'm in class, I just go off into Guyanese. . . . Yeah, especially if they have other Guyanese in the class.

Myrna George, 19, was born in Georgetown, the capital city of Guyana, but grew up in a rural village on the east coast of Guyana called Buxton. The sixth of seven children, Myrna has three brothers and three sisters. In Guyana, her father worked as a house painter and her mother earned a living as a small-scale trader. A soft-spoken teenager, Myrna often appeared to evade eye contact when being interviewed, which, in the context of Caribbean culture, might suggest respect for authority. I suspect, though, that in her case, shyness and nervousness might also be factors. Myrna's often sullen expression belied her warm, sensitive personality and understated sense of humor. She speaks in a slow, deliberate manner with a distinctly Guyanese accent. Based on her pronunciation, vocabulary, and syntax, Myrna can be characterized as a mesolect-dominant speaker whose language has been clearly influenced by a combination of rural residence and urban schooling in her native country and in the United States.

EARLY LANGUAGE AND SCHOOLING EXPERIENCES

In Buxton, where she grew up, Myrna said everyone spoke her native dialect, which she called *patois* (compare with Charles' term, *Creolese*). As mentioned in Chapter 2, Winford (1994) and Rickford (1987) note that rural/urban provenance is an important factor in determining speech varieties in Guyana. Myrna attended Friendship Primary School, located in the village adjacent to Buxton, and later, Christ Church Secondary School, a traditional academic high school located in Georgetown. She pointed out that teachers in her village did not pay much attention to her dialect. Only when she went to high school in Georgetown was her speech stigmatized. She admitted that she made a conscious effort to modify her accent when she went to school in Georgetown, for she was often teased about her rural accent by her urban high school peers: "Sometimes they tease me about it [her accent]...but it wasn't a problem. . . . Then after a year it changed. . . . I stopped talking like country." Yet, one of the most salient features of Myrna's pronunciation, usually associated with rural basilectal speech and often stigmatized, was her dropping of initial 'h' as evidenced in the following excerpts from one of her interviews with me:

Researcher: Did you have a chance to take the assignment home?
Myrna: We coulda take it 'ome.
Researcher: You felt that grade was okay?
Myrna: No, I thought it was gonna be 'igher.

Myrna's primary education was typical of that in other former British colonies in the Caribbean—a nationally controlled curriculum with a strong emphasis on essayist writing, especially strict adherence to the rules of prescriptive grammar. Reading usually consisted of short stories from a popular text, *The West Indian Reader*. Students were often asked to read aloud with a view to correcting "bad" (meaning Creole English) pronunciation—a practice being diminished, albeit slowly, by more progressive language policies and reading theory. After reading, students were asked to answer basic comprehension questions and/or write plot summaries of stories. Despite the limitations of this system, Myrna found pleasure in reading. She told me that she routinely borrowed books from the local library and enjoyed reading mysteries, especially the *Nancy Drew* and *Hardy Boys* series.

Myrna admitted that, at first, she felt her speech clearly influenced her writing, but once she began high school, she felt this was no longer the case. In high school in Guyana, Myrna wrote short stories and poems, and she claimed she did well on essays, finding them easier to write than essays in her New York City high school and at LIU. For one thing, "there were no drafts," she said, "we just write it one time, hand it in and that's it." This fundamental difference in approach to writing would become a challenge for Myrna in New York City schools.

MIGRATION AND SCHOOLING IN NEW YORK CITY

Like Charles, Myrna's family migration began with her uncle who sponsored her mother. Following the practice of staggered migration, Myrna's mother subsequently sponsored her (Myrna's) father, then the rest of the family. In May 1992, at age 15, Myrna, migrated to New York City. She and two of her sisters joined her parents who had already resided in the city for three years. Over the next four years, her remaining siblings would migrate and join the family. Like many Caribbean immigrants, Myrna arrived with mixed feelings of excitement and apprehension. After settling into her new neighborhood in East New York, she enrolled at Thomas Jefferson High School. Myrna was placed into the 10th grade, although according to her age and previous grade level, she should have been placed into the 11th grade. Neither Myrna nor her parents questioned her (mis)placement—a common practice among new Caribbean immigrants who are either unfamiliar with the American education system or afraid to challenge school authorities.

Myrna confessed that she was, at first, very conscious about her Guyanese accent, but as time went by, it became less important. Fortunately, neither her teacher nor her peers made an issue of her accent. In high school, her teachers were impressed by her writing, and so she was placed in the Honors English class, yet she admitted having difficulty with writing assignments. Teachers required more analysis and elaboration, writing practices that were unfamiliar to Myrna. She confessed having to rewrite papers because she was unclear what was being asked in the assignment. Here is her comparison of school writing in Guyana and New York City:

> Like back 'ome they give a subject, you 'ave to write on somet'ing—they just kind o' like look for the answer in the paper; but like over 'ere it's like more proofreading, like it gotta be more descriptive, more substance, more analysis, more examples . . . .

Myrna's frustration with her own writing was compounded by her perception that her grammar was weak. Her concern with grammar reflected a curious paradox. Although her early schooling in the Caribbean highly valued writing, the preoccupation with prescriptive grammar paradoxically often inhibited creative, meaningful writing. This reinforces Olson's (1977b) point that schools only really value one kind of writing—literate prose. Nonetheless, Myrna successfully completed her English classes in high school and graduated from Thomas Jefferson in June 1994.

WRITING AT LIU

In Fall 1994, Myrna began her tenure at LIU, planning to major in respiratory therapy. She was surprised when she was placed into English 13 at LIU. Despite her difficulties with English at Thomas Jefferson, she still perceived herself as an honors student. However, given the nature of the LIU placement test (it demands critical reading of a passage and an analytical response in essay form in a two-hour time frame), it is no surprise that Myrna had difficulty meeting the challenge. She had not been sufficiently apprenticed to the kinds of writing expected in a typical American college. Eleven years in the Guyanese educational system by far outweighed two years in a New York City high school.

DISCOURSE ANALYSIS

Myrna's writing over the course of four semesters might best be characterized as *academic interlanguage*—writing in flux, displaying features of both oral and written language, and various attempts to observe standard written English conventions. The genre and nature of writing assignments determined the degree to which she successfully approximated standard English.

Formal Writing

In English 13, most assignments were autobiographical or required narrative, descriptive kinds of writing, as the goal was to develop fluency in the inexperienced writer. However, Myrna's fluency at this level was seriously compromised by a tendency to write short declarative sentences beginning with the same pronoun. An excerpt from her essay on Judith Cofer's memoir about her bicultural life, *Silent Dancing*, illustrates this.

> A second 'moment of being' in Silent Dancing that is clear in Judith's mind, is when she was back in the United States of America, in the state of New Jersey. She was in elementary school. She didn't understand the English language. She wanted to go to the bathroom
> 5 but the teacher was not in the class at the time. She asked another

10 student, Puerto Rican as herself what she had to do to be excused. He told her that the writing on the board said, 'if you want to be excused simply write your name under the writing and you can go to the bathroom.' she then made her way towards the front of the room, but to stop short when she felt someone hit her over the head. She turned around only to realized that it was the teacher who had hit her in the head with a book.

Note that four successive sentences begin with "she," followed by one with "he," then two more with "she." The writing also reflects what Halliday (1989) describes as features of oral language, including frequency of verbs of action and feeling; for example, in lines 3-4: "she didn't understand," line 4: "she wanted," line 5: "she asked," lines 6-7: "he told her," lines 10-11: "she turned around." Although Myrna's purpose here was to describe a "moment of being," and to that degree the dynamic use of language was appropriate, her repetitive sentence structure weakened the effectiveness of the language as written discourse. Appropriate sentence combining could have facilitated fluency in this text.

However, in her autobiographical essay entitled "Unfair Competition in a Dishonest and Racist Society," Myrna's writing had a very different effect. In this essay, she described the experience of being discriminated against as a black person in a spelling bee competition in Guyana. Her opponents were students from a predominantly East Indian[4] school. The following is an excerpt from that essay (see Appendix C for full text):

I and two other students were picked to participate in the competition. On the day of the competition I woke up early approximately 6 a.m. Outside was still dark but the atmosphere was cool and refreshing. The swaying trees cast shadows across the wooden country house. Inside
5 the kitchen I could hear my mother hurrying about trying to prepare breakfast and get ready for work. I could hear my siblings half awoken by the sounds of pots and pans, asking what time it was.
I quickly hurried to the bathroom because I knew if my sister got their before I did, I would have to wait a long time and the last thing I
10 wanted to do was to show up late for my competition. I then got dressed in my brown uniform and beige jacket. I quickly munched on my breakfast and excused myself from the table after which I left for school. I was so excited to get to school.

Each student arrived early at school. We walked about half a mile to
15 reach the destination where the competition was held. As we made our way up the steps, we heard loud talking in the building, but as we entered the building the room grew into total silence and all eyes gazed on us.

66 CHAPTER SIX

> 20 Seats were left empty for us to sit, when we arrived. We quietly got seated. As soon as we were comfortable enough, the monitor announced the start of the competition. During the first part of the competition something unusual happened. The monitor gave a question and before he could finish the opposite buzzed in with the right answer. At first I thought it was just an intelligent guess, but after
> 25 awhile the same thing occurred. I knew at that instant that something was wrong. In some of the question you had to hear the end of it before you could gave the right answer.
>
> I began to realize what had happened. The monitor of the competition got at the competition site hours before the competition began. He was
> 30 East Indian and since the school was predominantly East indian he told many of the answers to the questions. I thought they were scared of us winning, because prior to that competition we had won over three other primary schools. At that moment I felt really angry. I tried to buzz in even if I didn't knew the answer.
>
> 35 Finally the competition ended and I was anxious to hear the results. The tension was rising in the room, my heart was thumping and although my teammates were silent I could sense that they were as nervous and anxious as I was. The judges returned with the score. My heart thumped faster and I began to sweat in the palm of my hands. My
> 40 foot began to shake, I began to bite my fingernails. I really felt nervous and uncomfortable.

The short sentences in this piece are very effective, for they build on each other to create a powerful narrative. By vividly describing events, people, places, and her own emotions, Myrna, like Charles in his autobiographical story, shows a high level of involvement, which is very effective here. There is an appeal to the senses, especially sight, sound, and feeling. We are told of the atmosphere: Outside it was "dark" but "cool and refreshing" . . . "swaying trees cast shadows across the wooden country house" (lines 3-4). Later, "[she] could hear [her] siblings half awoken by the sound of pots and pans" (line 6-7). Soon, the reader is drawn into Myrna's anxiety about the competition by her use of adverbs: "I quickly hurried to the bathroom", "I quickly munched on my breakfast."

On arrival at the competition site, Myrna captures the tension by contrasting "loud talking" (line 16) with "total silence" (line 17) as the opponents entered the room. She continues to build suspense in the narrative with sentences like "I knew at that instant that something was wrong" (lines 25-26) and "The tension was rising in the room" (line 36). Later, as the judges return with the score, the reader can feel the emotion of thumping hearts and sweating palms. Myrna's details are effective here because they are *real* indicators of nervousness. Given that the essay was based on a personal experience, she was able to write powerfully, making effective use of narrative devices of vivid description, appeal to the senses and building suspense, and widening her syntactic scope to include more adverbial and prepositional phrases. Myrna pointed out to me that she was very comfortable with and did well on autobiographical writing.

Essayist writing, however, demands other kinds of skills—writing that requires analysis, synthesis, and argumentation supported with clearly articulated evidence. In English 14, students were expected to move in this direction. Myrna's response to an essay by John (Fire) Lame Deer, a Sioux Native American, on the effect of technology on nature showed her grappling with more challenging writing. The following is an excerpt from her essay:

> John (Fire) Lame Deer, a sioux Native American, medicine man wrote an essay about nature entitled 'Talking to owls and butterflies.' He talks about how the white man's technology has changed the beautiful nature into a world of technology. Upon reading this essay I have
> 5 found that Deer made a few points that I agree with and a few that I totally disagree with.
>
> Deer said, 'The white man always pick the few unspoiled beautiful, awesome spots for the sites of these abomination.' The native Americans have lived, have survived on these lands, without
> 10 television, without lights, just living comfortably. They when by each day with what nature provided. Then came the white man and destroyed their homes. They build railroads on lands that the native Americans hunt and plant food. They build factories that was of no use to the native Americans whatsoever.
>
> 15 We must understand that the native Americans are born into this natural life. They are accustomed to hunting in the wild with bows and arrows, but the white man made it easier by inventing guns. They are born into homes without electricity, without pipes running into their homes, this was the life that they knew how to live. Deer said at the
> 20 beginning of his essay, he said that 'A good way to start thinking about nature, talk about it. Rather talk to it to the rivers, to the lakes, to the winds as to our relatives.' After reading this quote one can conclude the bond the native American had with nature.

I also agree with one of Deer's other points, saying that The terrible
25   arrogance of the white man making himself something more than god,
     more than nature, saying, 'I will let this live, because it make money;'
     saying, 'This animal must go it brings no income, the space it occupies
     can be use in a better way.' The white man has indeed thought of
     himself as god. Look at the issue of race, him saying that the white race
30   is superior over all other races. God has placed everything on this earth
     for a purpose even a wild animal man think should be destroyed
     because (as he said) has no purpose. What gave anyone the right,
     whether they are white or belong to any other ethnic group, to destroy
     a coyote that god placed on earth? People who are in power tend to
35   abuse their power when they destroy nature. Why is this? Obviously
     they think that they are God. Technology has made the white man so
     powerful that he just sees the world through technology and not
     through the Native Americans nature.

The subject of this essay is highly charged, and rather than assume the scholarly distance of an academic writer, Myrna appears to be taking the moral high ground. Abuse of nature and Native Americans is clearly stated as wrong. Yet, the verbal explicitness and elaboration needed in written discourse to support this position is noticeably absent. Instead, there is a presumption on Myrna's part that the audience agrees with her; consequently, there is no need for discussion. Myrna assumes a pro-Native-American position in the beginning of this essay without openly stating it. Only when she says in line 24, "I also agree with one of Deer's other points," the reader must infer that she agreed with all previously stated points. From here on, the writing takes on a sermonizing tone. Myrna charges unequivocally that "the white man has indeed thought of himself as god" (line 28-29). Her use of a rhetorical question in mid-text—"What gave anyone the right, whether they are white or belong to any other ethnic group to destroy a coyote that god placed on earth?" (lines 32-34)—is reminiscent of a pastor delivering a sermon. We see a language of absolutes: "We must understand that the native Americans are born into this natural life" (lines 15-16) or "Obviously they think that they are God" (lines 35-36). Bizzell (1984) asserts that such absolutes are at variance with academic discourse. Furthermore, there is no attempt to consider an alternative perspective. Most sentences are in the present indicative or the present perfect tense suggesting a kind of *fait accompli*. Shaughnessy (1977) contends that many basic writers substitute common wisdom for analysis when grappling with essayist writing. In this instance, Myrna appears to be going beyond common wisdom to preaching; thus, the writing takes on characteristics of oral language, for example, in lines 8-14, there is low lexical density (L:19; G: 42), frequency of parataxis, and less verbal explicitness based on the assumption of an accepting audience.

Later in the essay, Myrna attempts to take an opposing position by challenging Lame Deer and mounting a defense of modern technology. She charges that Deer's tone of voice and anger at the white man "makes his essay less convincing." The reader is taken by surprise by this sudden shift in argument, for Myrna does not utilize any of the conventional transitional devices that prepare the reader for such a shift (adverbial phrases such as "on the other hand" or "nevertheless"). The cohesive force of her argument is thus weakened (Halliday & Hasan, 1976). Instead, Myrna attacks Lame Deer in language that would be more appropriate if delivered orally: "He sounds selfish, talking about the native americans this, and the white man did that." This and that are vague references that might be acceptable in the here and now of oral language, but fall short of the explicitness demanded in essayist writing.

In the end, Myrna defends technology by arguing that it is not a deliberate attempt to destroy the world, but only to make life easier. After such a forceful anti-technology stance in the first half of the essay, the concession here seems almost contrived. One wonders if this was Myrna's attempt to preempt any possible challenge to her argument by her reader (in this case, the teacher) or merely her grappling with the rhetorical device of persuasion, taking on pros and cons within the same essay.

By English 16, Myrna began to show signs of internalizing more conventions of essayist writing. Most of her essays were organized around a standard frame—an introduction with a few general statements, a body addressing the specific details of the question reinforced with common wisdoms and a conclusion with more general statements. Whereas this is a common and acceptable frame in academia, it is not always appropriate for every writing assignment. Myrna seemed to organize the vast majority of her writing in this manner, finding a kind of safety zone in her academic interlanguage.

In one essay related to a short story, "Theft," by Joyce Carol Oates, Myrna began with an epigraph to contextualize the essay and later on in the text used quotations from Oates to support her points. These were clear indicators of her becoming apprenticed to essayist writing. Her writing at this level was markedly in flux, at once showing features of oral and written essayist language, with a greater tendency toward observing essayist conventions. She continued to employ mid-narrative questions as a rhetorical device in her essays; for example, "Do friends steal from each other? Do friends fight each other? I think not, not true friends." Allsopp (1979) points out that mid-narrative rhetorical questions are common features of Creole English speech as a means of sustaining the listener's attention. In writing, however, rhetorical questions are marked, for they are by definition oratory devices, which tend to abort argument and thus defy one of the principal conventions of essayist writing.

Self-Assessment: Portfolio Cover Letter

The portfolio cover letter is a unique text. It is at once the student's reflection on her own writing process and an attempt to make the best possible impression of herself and the writing program on the reader. By its very nature, it is formulaic. The following is an excerpt from Myrna's English 16 midterm portfolio cover letter:

> Dear readers:
>
> Reading and writing plays important roles in our everyday lives. Writing is expressing our inner thoughts on paper. It defines the way a person feels or think on a particular subject. It shows our weak and good areas. For some people oral communication and discussion is
> 5   easier than writing but for me writing is easier, I speak when I write.
>
> Before I begin writing, I would thoroughly read through the question, line by line before I begin my outline. I want to make sure that I really understand what the question is asking me to do. I do not want to make the mistake of giving information that the question didn't ask
> 10 for. I want to stick to the topic. I would then make my Plan-outline. My outline would include, my thesis sentence, and questions that I would answer in my essay. Sometimes I would read the question and I would not fully understand it. At night when I go to bed, I would lie in the dark thinking of how I would write my essay, how I would paragraph
> 15 it, and what quotes I would include in it.
> I enjoy quoting an author in my writings. It gives me a chance to elaborate on my thoughts on whatever the subject is. I would read a quote and then I would think about it, sometimes I would even fall in love with that quote. I would say to myself, 'This is exactly how I feel
> 20 but the quote have the perfect words.' Quoting an author helps me to express my thoughts more. I would analyze that quote and then write what I think it says.

Because a letter is a kind of oral text in writing, there are elements of both oral and written language displayed in the excerpt above. Myrna begins with features of written essayist language—use of nominalization, for example, "Reading" and "writing" are nominalized in line 1; greater lexical density in lines 1-5 (L:30; G:30). Immediately after she admits at the end of line 5, "I speak when I write," the writing begins to display features of oral language. There is an excessive use of the first person in the second paragraph—"I" is used 16 times in 17 clauses compared to two times in seven clauses in paragraph one. This provides a good example of Chafe and Danielewicz' (1987) point that letters tend to show the highest level of first person involvement.

In the first paragraph, the reader feels the third person distance prototypical of the essayist register whereas the second paragraph is consumed with the writer's agency. The language is also marked at times. In line 19-20 she says, "This is exactly how I feel but the quote have the perfect words." It is as if she gives agency to the quote to possess words.

In the latter half of the letter, there is a tremendous amount of repetition. Many sentences could be deleted, others combined. At times, Myrna's attempt to be "academic" results in odd word usage. She states, "I love revising my papers. I would add, subtract and substitute ideas into my paragraphs because I go off on my writing." Myrna might be unaware that "subtract" is restricted to the mathematical domain; "delete" would have been more appropriate. At the same time, "go off on my writing" sounds decidedly oral. Her final portfolio cover letter for English 16 was noticeably similar to her midterm letter and previous cover letters in form and content, which suggests that cover letters may have become for Myrna a formulaic exercise rather than a true process of reflecting on her own writing.

In-Class Writing

The effectiveness of Myrna's in-class writing depended on the nature of the text being responded to and the question she was responding to. In other formal writing assignments, there was ample time to discuss the assignment with the instructor and one's peers. In-class writing, however, demanded the ability to read and interpret both text and question and write a response in a limited time. In Myrna's case, if she was responding to a passage that included difficult, highly abstract concepts, she seemed to lose her voice. The writing then became very circular with chunks of highly sophisticated text being recycled then conjoined with her own simple sentences. When topics were more familiar and less abstract or the question itself created an essay frame, Myrna's writing was better. For example, she was able to write fluently on the advantages and disadvantages of computers.

At other times, Myrna used rhetorical questions and personalized the topic in order to take control of the writing, as evidenced in the following excerpt from a letter she wrote to Harriet Jacobs in response to Incidents in the Life of a Slave Girl:

> I have read your short story entitled, 'Incidents in the life of a slave girl'
> and I stumbled on one of your quote that I so much believe in,
> 'degraded by the system that has brutalized her.'
> I wasn't born during slavery, and I'm so happy I didn't but in the
> 5 society in which I live, I have not only observe someone being
> 'degraded by a system that has brutalized them' but I have also
> experienced it. As a young black woman I have to cope with prejudice
> and hate. In today society there are do's and don't's because of the color
> of your skin, for example a black man driving a expensive, nice car may
> 10 be stop by the police because he black, and blacks are not expected to
> live in luxury, only if he's a drug dealer or some type of criminal. A
> black man or woman cannot play golf, only if he is rich and famous.
> Do you think blacks deserve this? Do you think anyone deserves this?
> African Americans did not ask to come to the United States but were
> 15 brought here by force. Our ancestors have survived their brutalities.
> They've lived with the beatings, hunger, the emotional stress. Why is
> the system degrading them now? Haven't they brutalized them
> enough? How much more can one take?

In lines 5-8, Myrna brings to the text her personal experience of prejudice as a direct result of slavery. She takes control of the writing by citing real-life examples of black men today being discriminated against because of their race (lines 8-11) and she poses two rhetorical questions to Jacobs (line 13), the first being reinforced by the repetition in the second: "Do you think blacks deserve this? Do you think anyone deserves this?" The second person <u>you</u> in these questions gives the impression that Myrna is speaking to Jacobs. It is as if Jacobs were alive and able to respond orally to her questions. In fact, Myrna poses three more rhetorical questions to Jacobs (lines 16-18) in an effort to underscore the seriousness of the issue. Because Myrna appears to be "speaking" to Jacobs on slavery, a topic about which she is very passionate, the letter presents a good example of an oral text in writing.

Research Paper

English 17 presented a formidable challenge for Myrna. She confessed that it was her first attempt at writing an academic research paper. Her project was a semester-long investigation of a community-based organization in her neighborhood. It included an oral history documenting one person's involvement in a local community group and also secondary research that would frame the oral history in a broader context.

Myrna was able to complete successfully the first part of the project, which was the oral history. She conducted a tape-recorded interview with a representative of a community-based organization. Her oral history described the goals and activities of the organization, its role in the community, the interviewee's role in the organization, and Myrna's own reflections on what she learned from the interview:

> United community centers Inc. is an organization in the East New York area of Brooklyn. Since I am a resident of this district I felt obligated to find out as much as I could about this organization. I felt responsible because I live in East New York for almost five years and I
> 5 never knew this organization existed until now. I decided to interview someone from this organization, someone with great knowledge on the organization. I interviewed Ana Agairra, the director of the organization....
> United community centers came into being about forty years ago. It
> 10 started out as being many centers but then the centers came together, they united to form one center. It was founded by the tenants association of the neighborhood. Ana said:
>> uh so a lot of tenants, they wanted to get together and have a center and initially it wasn't a formal way, that's why they called it united
> 15 because a lot of people get together and have an informal center after awhile it become formal you know with rules and approval by the city.
> As I listen to Ms agairra talk of how the center came into effect a warm feeling came over me. I felt really happy because it showed that the
> 20 tenants really cared about the community. They united, came together became stronger to make a difference. As most of us know it is very hard to get support from members of the community and the government to form an organization.
> UCCI is an non-profit organization which means most of its workers
> 25 are volunteers. Many of the volunteers are high school students who volunteer during their summer vacations....This organization functions to meet the needs of the community. It provides a day care center for the kids of the community.

When Myrna attempted to incorporate secondary material into her research, however, the writing changed considerably. Instead of combining elements of primary and secondary material to support a central thesis, she inserted all secondary material into the first half of the paper. The oral history then followed in the manner of an addendum with an unclear relation to the secondary material. It appears that Myrna's difficulty with the project stemmed from her not grasping the point of secondary research. In other words, why was there a need to put the oral history in a larger social context? In the syllabus for the course, Myrna's instructor stipulated that "the final paper will be a compilation of primary and secondary material"—a difficult combination for a novice researcher like Myrna to manage successfully. The result was that the first three paragraphs of her final draft became a lesson in the history of East New York with no documentation of sources. The following is the beginning of her paper:

> Where is East New York? Who founded this great city? Who occupied it in the past and who occupies it now? When doing research on my community these questions surfaced in my mind. I want my readers to really understand and get to know my community.
>
> 5   In the late 1830's up until the 1860's the accelerated growth of East New York was due to the settlement of the Germans. They added to the predominant population of Dutch, small group of English and Irish, who settled in New Lots a small part of East New York.
>
> After the Dutch settled then came the settlers from the East who
> 10 moved across the country searching for towns. John R. Pitkin, a connecticut Yankee, a far sighted business man and a man with a vision for the village of New lots, visited the village. He was impressed with the lands lying between the hills north of Jamaica Bay on the south side and he began to dream. He dreamt of finding a great city that
> 15 would rival New York. John R. Pitkin founded the village of East New York. In the past East New York was predominantly a white neighborhood but at the years progressed Blacks and Hispanics moved in and Whites moved out.

With the exception of lines 1 to 4 immediately above, most of the language in this section of the paper does not appear to be Myrna's. The three questions in lines 1-2 and the first-person sentence "I want my readers to really understand and get to know my community" (lines 3-4) are decidedly different from the fact-based sentences in lines 5-6 and 9-10. It is likely that beginning in line 5 the text is plagiarized from a history textbook or encyclopedia. I am not suggesting that Myrna's plagiarism was deliberate. Rather, I believe it might have been a function of being an inexperienced researcher and not really understanding what constitutes plagiarism.

Furthermore, the difference in the writing between the oral history and the section with secondary sources is reflected in the lexical density. In the oral history, the first 200 words have a lexical density of L: 57; G: 143 (28%), compared to L: 87; G: 113 (43%) for the same number of words in the section with secondary sources. More specifically, within the latter, the lexical density in lines 1-4 is L: 13; G: 33 (28%) compared to L: 21; G: 25 (46%) in lines 5-8. The statistics on lexical density in regard to Myrna's research paper reveal a similar pattern to Charles' paper whereby higher lexical density seems to be related to plagiarism. The overall lexical density of 400 words in Myrna's research paper is L: 144; G: 256 (36%). Like Charles, Myrna's type/token ratio—184/400 or .46—also suggests a generally narrow range of lexical items, despite the possible plagiarism.

In examining the level of verbal explicitness in Myrna's research paper, I was struck by her tendency to be repetitive, often redundant, especially in the oral history. Myrna seemed very focused on making her ideas clear to her reader, resulting in several instances of repetition. For example, in the oral history section, line 2: "Since I am a resident of this district" is the same idea as line 4: "because I live in East New York." In line 6, the repetition of "someone" could have been avoided by the use of the relative pronoun "who." In lines 10-11, "came together" and "united" are redundant. The repetition of "centers" in line 10 could have been replaced with pronouns. The same holds true for the repetition of "volunteers" in line 25. Myrna seems to equate elaboration (one way to achieve verbal explicitness) with repetition. Although the former might include the latter, elaboration could also be achieved by illustration or explication of ideas.

The abovementioned section of Myrna's research paper was analyzed on a morphosyntactic level and the results are summarized in Table 3.

Table 3. Morphosyntactic Features. Total Number of Morphosyntactic Errors in 400 Words of Myrna's Research Paper.

	Actual Occurrences	Possible Occurrences
Verb-Related Features		
Zero inflection for:		
third person singular	0	6
past tense	4	38
verb particles	1	3
Total:	5	47

Table 3 shows that Myrna's research paper revealed errors only in verb-related areas. The low occurrence of error might be attributed to the fact that a portion of her paper appeared to have been plagiarized. Still, the presence of verb-related errors in her research paper was consistent with the qualitative analysis done on the rest of her writing, which revealed many verb-related errors, especially instances of overgeneralization. The following are examples of error from Myrna's writing in English 13 to 16:

Subject-Verb Concord

Missing third person -s

1. A moment of being is when someone experience* something that leave* a lasting impression in their life.
2. Television advertisement play* a role by training the people to accept conditions as destiny in that it show* them only the best part of life.
3. When someone read* my work, they should feel the need to go on until the end.

Intrasentential distraction of subject

1. Writing much essay have* helped me.
   The plurality of "much essay" (many essays) being so close to the verb induces a plural subject/verb concord, and distracts the real subject, "writing", which requires the third person singular form of the verb.
2. The Indians' freedom were* taken away from them.
   Again the plurality of Indians distracts from the singularity of freedom.

Zero Inflection

For past tense

If the context already indicates past action. Both Roberts and Holm claim this is a typical Creole English feature:

1. When reading it the second time, I underline* a few paragraphs.
   (<u>Second time</u> already suggests past tense).

In the absence of a clear contextual indicator of past action, past tense may be marked only on the first verb of a sentence. Subsequent markings for past are seen as redundant. In a sense, the first inflection sets up a past tense context:

1. I never wrote much before I attend* LIU.
2. Robby didn't care what people think* of him.

For participles

Passive structures are not part of Creole English syntax. The inflection needed on the participle to complete the passive structure in standard English tends to be omitted in Creole English.

1. The only time I would write a paper is if it was assign* to the class.
2. A black man driving a expensive car can be stop* by the police.
3. This gives me a chance to see whether or not my paper is address* to its readers.

Compound verb phrases

1. I have not only observe* someone being degraded by the system that brutalized them, but I have also experience* it.
2. Have you ever wonder* how they suffer?
3. I was a little disappointed to what I had encounter*.

Plurals

Omission of plural -s when noun preceded by determiner that indicates the noun is plural. Determiners are underlined.

1. <u>These</u> moment* are so peculiar that they are out of her everyday experience.
2. Judith Cofer and Virginia Woolf are writer* of <u>two</u> book* of memoirs.
3. <u>Both</u> party* must know what was going to happen next.

Omission of -s when count nouns in generic form

1. Citizen* constantly live in fear.
2. In high school, we would write essay* on a regular basis.
3. Computer* can be used for a good many thing*.

In strictly morphosyntactic terms, the examples immediately above may not be issues of plurality. Generic count nouns are seen as singular or collective entities, and their -s inflection might be simply a matter of prescriptive grammar convention. For Myrna, the omission of the -s is consistent with the Creole English feature of zero inflection, or perhaps she may be unaware of the standard English rules for marking generic count nouns.

Overgeneralization of Standard English Rules

For third person -s

1. I understand I cannot change the way the people in the world feels*.
2. They provides* extracurricular activity and counseling for the people in the neighborhood.
3. Many of the residents in this community does* not realize how important this organization is.

For past tense

In attempting to move away from the Creole English tendency toward zero inflection and to observe standard English rules, Myrna often overcompensates.

1. A Puerto Rican boy came to admired* her on his bike.
2. I didn't knew* the answer.
3. Did the Indians asked* to be taught Christianity?

Phonological Influence on Spelling

In addition to the above features, three instances of phonological influence on spelling were found. Two involved omission of initial "h," a feature observed earlier in Myrna's speech.

1. Writing journal entry as* helped me to understand the book much better.
2. Being in English 100 at LIU as* been both a challenge and an interesting experience.
3. One would one* [want] to maintain the abyss between the well-being of some and the misery of others.

It should be pointed out that there was no instance of omission of initial "h" in the word <u>have</u>. This may be due to the fact that <u>ave</u> is clearly not a standard English word whereas <u>as</u> is; thus, Myrna might not have recognized <u>as</u> as an error. It is well to note also that whereas zero copula in certain syntactic environments is a very prominent feature in Creole English, Myrna's writing showed no evidence of this. Perhaps, the absence of copula is such a stigmatized feature that Myrna might have been careful to observe standard English rules when using it. There was also no evidence of Creole English usage of standard English grammatical words in Myrna's writing.

FINAL REFLECTIONS

After four years in the United States, Myrna was still very much aware of her speech patterns and Guyanese accent, especially in the classroom. She felt there was a "big difference" between the way she spoke at home and with her friends and the way she spoke in class (she usually adjusted her speech toward standard English in class as many Creole English speakers did). However, with the increasing number of anglophone Caribbean students at LIU, Myrna admitted to lapsing into "Guyanese" sometimes in class. She said, "Sometimes, when I'm talking in class, I just go off into Guyanese. . . . Yeah, especially if they have other Guyanese in the class."

Reflecting on her writing over four semesters, Myrna seemed to have mixed feelings, as seen in the following sequence:

Researcher: Do you feel or see any difference in your writing from English 13 to English 17?
Myrna: No, to me is the same t'ing. You know I didn't know why I do 13 and 14 and 16 and 17 'cause it's the same t'ing. So I t'ink dey shoulda jus' put me in 16 and 17 'cause you know it's the same process o' writin'.
Researcher: So you didn't really see any big differences?
Myrna: No, except 17—probably the research paper 'cause I never did dat, but 16 was the same t'ing as 14 and 13. So it don' make sense.

English 17 was Myrna's first attempt at writing a research paper—a new type of discourse. Following Gee's (1990) discourse theory, to become apprenticed to the research genre, Myrna must think and act like a researcher. This meant learning techniques of time management, finding, skimming and scanning secondary materials, making informed choices on which materials to integrate into her paper, developing a focused thesis, and correctly documenting sources. In her commentary on the project, Myrna stated,

> As a researcher, thinker, reader and writer, I learned How to arrange time, place and articles. How to schedule the way I would go about my research. I also learned how to skim through materials to find what was going to be beneficial to me in writing. I thought a lot of the way I would integrate my material into my narrative.
>
> Although it was difficult at times finding information for my secondary research, it was kind of fulfilling. Interviewing and transcribing were all so new to me but I can say these are a few of the things I learned to do. I am happy that I learned so much about the research process because I know it would be helpful in the future.

Myrna's perception of her research process might have been at odds with what she actually did. Yet, such inconsistencies are a part of any apprenticeship. She *did* learn to conduct and transcribe an interview. To that extent, the process was successful. However, Myrna's instructor felt that her paper was indeed plagiarized. To resolve the matter, the instructor gave her an "incomplete" grade for the course and suggested that she work with a tutor over the summer to come to a better understanding of research and working with secondary sources.

Still, Myrna told me that she felt she *did* make some progress, especially in analyzing texts, quoting, summarizing, and proofreading. However, she continued to have concerns about her grammar, especially subject/verb concord: "I always have to do work on my grammar" she said, "and yeah, sometimes I still write the way I speak."

7

Nadine Ferguson

> We weren't allowed to speak patois, not in school. . . . Yeah, in my home, too. I wasn't allowed to speak like that.

Nadine Ferguson was a chatty, bright-eyed 19-year-old with a cheerful personality. Born in 1977 in Kingston, the capital city of Jamaica, Nadine had fond memories of her tropical island home, living with her older brother, her mother who was a nurse, and her father, a furniture maker. But her happy childhood was suddenly interrupted one day in August 1982, when her mother migrated permanently to the United States leaving her and the rest of the family behind in the care of an older female guardian. Nadine's mother eventually sponsored the family, who joined her in New York City four-and-a-half years later.

Having migrated at age nine, Nadine's Jamaican accent had somewhat faded, except for an incipient musicality that is typical of Caribbean speech. However, in moments of excitement or on highly emotional topics, her accent became more pronounced. A conscientious student who was meticulous about her work, Nadine planned to major in nursing.

EARLY LANGUAGE AND SCHOOLING EXPERIENCES

In Jamaica, Nadine attended Yallahs Primary School in the parish of St. Thomas. She recalled that her home language, which she characterized as *patois* or *broken English*, was forbidden in school. She added, ironically, that she was not allowed to speak patois in her home either. Following is an excerpt from our conversation on this issue:

Researcher: Back in Jamaica, how did they deal with the dialect in school?
Nadine: Actually, we weren't allowed to speak patois, not in school.
Researcher: Oh, really?
Nadine: Yeah, in my home, too. I wasn't allowed to speak like that. Only when I was outside with my friends we spoke like that. . . . Sometimes my mother doesn't wanna hear it, but *she* speaks like that, too!. . . . 'Cause she thinks I might take it outside the house.

In other words, despite her natural speech, Nadine was being trained to think of herself not as a Creole English speaker but as a native speaker of standard English. To appease her mother, Nadine assured her that she did not speak the dialect in the classroom, only socially with her friends. Not only was Nadine's mother opposed to the vernacular, but the female guardian in whose care Nadine was left also disapproved of the use of Jamaican Creole English at home. As Nadine put it, "My family, they don't talk like that [meaning Jamaican Creole], and the lady who my mom left to take care of us, *she* didn't allow me to speak like that either." The comments here reflect the paradox of the Caribbean linguistic situation where the mass vernacular is often stigmatized by its own speakers.

Nadine's earliest recollections of reading in school were mostly of pattern drills like "See Sally Run." She also remembered going to her neighborhood library and reading books with pictures or stories of Jamaica. Writing was focused on prescriptive grammar exercises, but Nadine found her own pleasures by writing letters to her mother in New York City.

MIGRATION AND SCHOOLING IN NEW YORK CITY

After migrating to New York City in December 1986, Nadine had very little time to adjust to her new home in Cambria Heights, for she immediately began school at P.S. 136, a junior high school in Queens. She recalled feeling "excited" on her first day at school in New York. Many students wanted to befriend her, "'cause they never met a Jamaican. . . . They didn't know much about Jamaicans." Although some students wanted her to "talk Jamaican," others made fun of her accent. This made her very self-conscious about her speech, especially her pronunciation of initial "h," which, as already noted, is a stigmatized Creole feature. Nadine discussed her speech below:

Researcher: So were you self-conscious about your accent?
Nadine: Yeah, that's probably why I don't like English 'cause in English class you have to read out loud and I never like that.
Researcher: Because you feel your accent . . .
Nadine: Yes, that they'll laugh.
Researcher: But you don't have much of an accent now though.
Nadine: Well, the aitches!! (laughter by both researcher and Nadine) I have to think before I say it . . . like when I'm about to say a word that begins with "h," I have to think about it so that I can pronounce it when it's needed and not when it's not needed.

After graduating from P.S. 136, Nadine attended Andrew Jackson High School in Queens. She noted that there were many Jamaican students at Jackson and, like Charles, pointed to the hostility between Caribbean, especially Jamaican, and American students:

That high school was full o' them [Jamaicans]. . . . Oh yes, the end of the year, it was like Jamaicans against Americans. It was crazy. . . . I mean physical fight. . . . Because it was so many o' them, they felt they had power or something.

Nadine believed that the abundance of Jamaicans at Jackson, coupled with the presence of a stepsister who came to live with her family and who had mostly Jamaican friends, brought out her Jamaican dialect: "Just around that time, it [the Jamaican dialect] just came right back."

In high school, Nadine was placed in the <u>Diploma to Degree</u> program—an accelerated program for promising students, which condensed the four-year high school sequence into three years and guaranteed students a place at LIU upon graduation. Nadine admitted that there was "a lot of pressure" in the program and that English class was an unpleasant experience: "It was two periods at the end of the day," she lamented, "and we just wanted to go *home*" (her emphasis). In English, she read many of the classics—Greek mythology, Shakespeare, *The Scarlet Letter* and *Lord of the Flies* to name a few. Writing was largely done as a one-shot exercise. Only in her last year in high school was Nadine introduced to writing drafts. When asked if she felt her speech influenced her writing in high school, her response was:

> It used to. . . . Yeah, but English 13 and 14 . . . it kinda taking it out of it. 'cause I used to write exactly how I speak . . . 'cause I won't say Jamaicans are backwards but some of those words like 'new brand' pants instead of 'brand new'—it's kinda strange.

WRITING AT LIU

In the fall of 1994 Nadine began classes at LIU. Unlike Myrna, Nadine's placement into English 13 was no surprise to her. She admitted that she had difficulty writing under pressure and did not fare well on what she referred to as "those tests" [meaning placement tests or any type of writing under similar conditions]. In fact, at the end of English 13, Nadine tried to be exempted from English 14 by retaking the placement test, but was unsuccessful. Reflecting on the retake exam, she said,

> The professor gave me the chance to see if I could go to English 16, and I still did poorly . . . and I think I coulda did better. . . . I don't know, it could be the nervousness. I don't like taking those tests.

For this reason, Nadine disliked in-class writing as well.

Most of Nadine's writing, both formal and informal, reflected her attempt to adhere to standard English rules and observe conventions of essayist writing. Having migrated to New York City at an early age, Nadine had been immersed in an environment of American English speakers. She therefore had more time and opportunity to develop both receptive and productive skills in standard American English while being less influenced by Creole English.

DISCOURSE ANALYSIS

Formal Writing

In the early stages of Nadine's college career, her writing consisted of many simple sentences with few relative clauses. She did attempt to do some amount of analysis. Following is an excerpt from a draft of her first essay in English 13 on Judith Cofer's *Silent Dancing*:

> It was under the mango tree that Cofer 'first began to feel the power of words.' The significance of this 'moment of being' in Cofer's life is that

> she looks up to the women in her family, such as her mother,
> grandmother, and aunts. They served as role models for her. Cofer
> 5   observed the routines of the women in her life. This way she got an
> understanding of the role that women played in her society. This
> moment might have given Cofer a sense that her family is of great
> value, particularly the strong women characters who served as her role
> models.

The sentences in lines 2-6 might have been combined to read, "By observing the routines of women in her life, Cofer began to understand the role of women in her society." Still, Nadine must be credited with going beyond a mere retelling of the story and attempting to explain the significance of a particular moment of being. Later in the essay, she tries to place these 'moments of being' in a larger context of human experience:

> <u>Silent Dancing</u> contains many different 'moments of being.' This was
> just one of the many moments in Cofer's life, that molded her into
> who she is today; a successful teacher and writer. Virginia Woolf
> believes the characteristics of all childhood memories account for an
> 5   individual's strenght in the future. Everyone's life reflects their
> moments in the past, whether they are exceptional or not.
> Psychologists can often identify one's past experiences by studying the
> behavior.

Although the central idea of the paragraph above concerns the influence of one's past on one's future, the shifting of sentence-initial subject in lines 3-7 blurs a clear anaphoric reference, thereby weakening the cohesiveness of the writing (Halliday & Hasan, 1976). Moving from "Virginia Woolf" to "Everyone's life" to "Psychologists" in three successive sentences does not allow sufficient development of the idea(s) in any one sentence. For example, in the first draft of this essay, Nadine's instructor questioned what she meant by "the characteristics of all childhood memories" (line 4). Nadine never addressed the instructor's question in her revision, which suggests she might have felt that her intended meaning was sufficiently articulated or she might not have been proficient enough in essayist explication at this stage to elaborate on her points.

When writing her autobiographical essay, however, Nadine was quite adept at manipulating language. Inspired by Cofer's integration of Spanish and English in *Silent Dancing*, Nadine effectively incorporated Jamaican Creole English into her essay, "Too Close for Comfort," as she described the experience of her mother's leaving Jamaica and then returning later to bring her and her brother to the United States. The following is an excerpt from that essay:

86 CHAPTER SEVEN

August 28, 1982 my mother left my brother and me. At the airport in Jamaica, I was very serious and not smiling. It was one week after my birthday. 'Chu Chu, Mommy going away for two weeks. I'll bring back a lot of things for you.' I stood there speechless and serious. I had always
5 been a serious child.

In kindergarten, my teacher spank me.
'Mommy, Miss Dunkan lick me and mi nuh trouble har.'
'Teachers always hit children in order for them to learn.'
'Mi nah go back a school, mi Nanny a fi teach mi a yard.'
10 My mother left Jamaica and four years later she returned.

It was November of 1986 that my life took a turn. It was a Monday, a regular school day for me. This particular day I walked home alone. I entered my yard. I began to notice that all my neighbors were staring. 'What happened?'
15 'Nothing [Nadine].'
As I stepped into the house, I noticed that there was a woman sitting at my dining table. The face was familiar but I was still puzzled. There was a picture above her. The picture was of my mother. I looked at the picture, then I looked at the woman.

20 '[Nadine], do you remember me?'
'Yes Mommy.' Then we hugged. A month later, my brother and I were brought to the United States. I was nine and my brother thirteen.

In the first three lines, the reader is immediately drawn into Nadine's feelings of abandonment. Her mother left one week after her (fifth) birthday. Her sentences are short but explicit: "I stood there speechless and serious. I had always been a serious child" (lines 4-5). Later, in lines 7-9, Nadine contrasts her Creole English speech with her mother's standard English response, suggesting the mother's subtle disapproval of Creole English by modeling standard English. On the whole this is very effective writing.

When Nadine's mother returns to Jamaica four years later, we learn by inference that "Mommy going away for two weeks" (line 3) was not true. Nadine could barely recognize her mother after the four-year absence. Only when she looks at the picture above the dining table, then looks at the woman sitting below it, does she make the connection. The imagery here is powerful and the reader is drawn into the emotion of the moment.

The writing in this essay changed when Nadine attempted to place her immigrant status in a broader social context, an idea evidently suggested by her writing instructor. She wrote:

> The 'politics of marginalization' is a term that Dorothy Allison describes in her work, A question of class. I will use this concept to show where my family fit in. The centre mainly consists of those who are middle-class whites, and the rich. On the margin are women,
> 5 immigrants, the poor, and minorities. My family can be located on the margin. We are all minorities. Some of us are women and some immigrants. Most of my mother's sisters and their children are abroad. They now reside in England, Canada and the United States.

In the excerpt above, Nadine attempts to render her interpretation of the "politics of marginalization," a term that is apparently new to her and seems out of step with the narrative writing of the first half of this essay. The writing at this point begins to increase in lexical density—(L: 40; G: 40) in the excerpt above compared to (L: 31; G: 49) for the first 80 running words of the essay. But the level of abstraction needed to sustain a discussion on the "politics of marginalization" seems to be too much for Nadine. She reverts to short, simple sentences, for example, "We are all minorities. Some of us are women and some immigrants" (lines 6-7), for the ideas are too complicated for her to handle. In the end, she veers away from marginalization by discussing her own process of Americanization and the conflicts this created on her last vacation to Jamaica. (See Appendix D for full text.)

One of the conflicts Nadine faced in her attempt to approximate essay writing was her desire to follow the instructor's guidelines. Nadine pointed out that she felt the need for guidelines in order to do essay writing assignments, yet guidelines often confused her. Many times she did four or five drafts of the same essay, trying to approximate what she thought the instructor wanted. This was the case in her English 14 essay on John Hersey's *Hiroshima*, a book about the survivors of the 1945 atomic bomb in Japan. Nadine wrote five drafts of this essay, spending much of her time retelling the stories of the survivors while her instructor kept prompting her in each draft to make her "point" or discuss the "issue." In other words, Nadine was being pushed to meet a fundamental requirement of essayist writing—a focus on highlighting important issues and explaining their significance. Below is an excerpt from one draft of this essay followed by some of her instructor's comments:

> After the bomb, the survivors tried to cope with the situation the best they could. Some had more faith than others. Sasaki did not handle things well. After the bomb she had little interest in living, because she could not believe that God would allow such thing to happen to
> 5 innocent people. When she was found by some friends, she received the news that her brother might have died. Miss Sasaki soon found out

that her baby brother might have died because he was in the hospital that collapsed. She also found out later that her fiancé's family had 'second thoughts about permitting their son to marry a 'Hibakusha'
10   and a cripple.' Her parents left her some savings and she used it to take up sewing to help support her sister and her brother. She placed them in an orphanage and later worked there to be with them.

Instructor's comments on the paragraph above:
(1) What is the main point you're trying to make about Ms. Sasaki?
(2) Put this all in a specific framework.
(3) What was her main survival issue?

Summative comments:
(1) Don't just give facts; explain their significance.
(2) Explain how each character was forever changed by the catastrophe.

By the final draft, Nadine attempted to respond to the instructor's comments by showing how each character was permanently changed:

Social and natural catastrophes always have a lasting impact on the individuals who experienced them. Their lives are never the same as before. They usually begin to value life more. Each of the individuals mentioned coped with the tragedy differently. Sasaki did not have
5   much faith in God, but in the end, her identity changed drastically. She gave her soul to God. Nakamura gained more strength by raising her children and helping them to survive....

Mr. Tanimoto became a spokesperson. Travelling to the states influenced him. He became even more concerned with other's
10   well-being. He not only preached the word of God to those who needed it, but he also helped a group of girls who were physically destroyed by the bomb. Uncle Lorenzo is near retirement, right now he still preaches and visits the United States to get the things for the poor. Aunty Carmen is now stronger than ever, because she works hard to
15   support her children by herself. Today Dudley looks at life differently, he turned himself around and is now a strong believer in God. These survivors all struggled to make the best out of their situation and accomplished their goals in the end.

Nadine noted that her writing was better when she had some control over the assignment. We see evidence of this in English 16 when she was asked to choose a printed advertisement, describe and analyze it in terms of the stereotypes it presented. Nadine chose an ad for an antihistamine, Benadryl Elixir, taken from *Episodes*, a popular soap opera magazine. The ad showed a group of five children from different ethnic groups dressed in lab coats, posing as medical doctors. A bottle of Benadryl sat at the lower right corner of the ad. Because Nadine chose the ad herself, she had ample time to examine its text and subtext and to write a more careful analysis of its message. She wrote:

> Stereotypes that deal with gender, race and class are depicted in this ad. The way each child is presented is proof of this. For years, the color pink has been associated with girls. 'Dr. Diane's' nametag is pink, but the boys' nametags are blue. The pink is associated with girls from
> 5   birth. It represents someone who is vulnerable and fragile....Another point is that the ad depicts three males and two females. The females are 'sandwiched' by the males, as though the males are their bodyguards....
>
> 'Dr. Tim' is wearing a yellow shirt that matches his hair, and a black tie.
> 10 The tie has blue stripes with thin gold-looking stripes. There is no doubt about it: This boy represents the wealthy white doctors of our society....This ad deliberately appeals to minorities, offering them a sad fantasy of equality. Years ago, this kind of product would have been advertised with a mother and her sick child being tucked in. This is a
> 15 victory, not for equality, but for advertising.

Nadine's writing in the excerpt above shows the verbal explicitness and analysis needed in essayist writing. She begins the paragraph with the topic sentence: "Stereotypes that deal with gender, race and class are depicted in the ad," then she proceeds to elaborate on each aspect of the sentence. She explains how stereotypes of girls are depicted in the ad by pointing out that the girls are framed as "vulnerable and fragile" (line 5) because they appear to be protected (sandwiched) by the males "as though the males are their bodyguards" (lines 7-8). Nadine also analyzes the stereotypes associated with certain colors—pink for girls, blue for boys—and explains their significance in terms of how each boy and girl in the ad is perceived. She notes that "Dr. Tim's" yellow shirt and black tie with blue and gold stripes give him a serious look. His authority as a doctor is not to be questioned: "There is no doubt about it. This boy represents the wealthy white doctors of our society" (lines 10-12). Nadine suggests that it is no coincidence that, among the kids in the ad, the white boy is to be taken the most seriously. Finally, she analyzes the subtext of the ad—its appeal to minorities. She is able to detect that the ethnic mix in the ad is alluring but offers a "sad fantasy of equality" (lines 12-13). The different and unequal representations of ethnicity by the boys and girls in the ad contradict its own putative message of equality. Nadine concludes that the ad is a victory not for racial equality but for advertising.

Yet, in the same course, she had difficulty maintaining clarity when she had less control of the assignment. In an essay on Patra, a Jamaican reggae singer, she tried to incorporate words such as "matriarchal hegemony" from the instructor's assignment. One sentence read thus: "Patra offers some girls the opportunity to find meanings of their own feminine sexuality that they can handle, meanings that are of matriarchal hegemony." Like the "politics of marginalization," "matriarchal hegemony" appeared to be a performance of instructor-induced language and, in fact, hindered rather than helped clarity in the sentence.

In-Class Writing

Nadine admitted that in-class writing was her least favorite. Many of her in-class writing assignments entailed grappling with abstract subjects in a limited amount of time. Nadine did not fare well in these circumstances. Her writing typically became circular and difficult to understand at several points. Here is an example from an essay on Dorothy Allison's A Question of Class: "There will always be those who are superior because of royal families and gambling. No two people are alike so there will always be class stratification, racism and prejudice." It is difficult for the reader to make a connection between "royal families and gambling." Furthermore, the second sentence does not help to clarify the first.

In another essay on Mary Louise Pratt's Arts of the Contact Zone, Nadine repeated many of Pratt's words verbatim but then conjoined them with an overly simplified explanation: "Pratt mentions the place of unsolicited oppositional discourse, parody, resistance and critique. . . . She mean that there are opinions that are shared and everyone does not share the same opinion." As can be seen, such conjoining does not work well, as I pointed out when discussing Myrna's writing.

Portfolio Cover Letter

Nadine's English 16 portfolio cover letter was an honest assessment of her reading and writing processes. She admitted her own difficulty with analysis:

> Upon entering English 16, my goal was to be more analytical when reading. My problem was understanding what the writer is trying to

> put across to the reader. At times, it was hard for me to distinguish between the writer's views from that of others. . . . The in-class essay that is included in my portfolio is not one of my best piece because there was insufficient time to complete the assignment. . . . I was not able to reflect on my thoughts and organize my information into a complete essay.

It should be noted that the cover letter itself shows that Nadine had, in fact, internalized patterns of organization. The first half of the letter addressed her reading issues and the second half focused on writing—first essays, then in-class writing. At that stage, she had learned to develop an idea across several sentences, a noticeable change from English 13.

Informal Writing: Journals

The following represent two samples of Nadine's journal writing:

> <u>From English 13</u>
> This class is not as bad as I thought it would be. This is because their are a lot of outspoken people in here. The work seems okay, but I wish the break was longer. I no longer feel intimidated when I speak. . . . I have a few questions—why are we only reading autobiographies? why do we get so much unnecessary written assignments?

Nadine's lighthearted tone and brutal honesty here are appropriate for journal writing. One can imagine her telling the excerpt above to someone. The rhetorical questions, as noted earlier, are markers of casual oral language.

> <u>From English 14</u>
> Nuclear wars and weapons are very dangerous. They can destroy thousands of people's lives within minutes. I do not know all the facts behind Hiroshima but I do know it was wrong. How can one take so many innocent lives and destroy the future of the rest? This makes me look at the United States as being wicked.

Nuclear war is a highly charged topic. Like Myrna's essay on the destruction of nature, the topic lends itself to a moralizing tone. This environment is ripe for the rhetorical question in lines 3-4.

Research Paper

Nadine's research project was conducted on a community based after-school program called *Safe Harbor After School Recreation Program* (SHARP). This program was offered at P.S. 136, the junior high school that Nadine attended, so she was investigating familiar territory. In her proposal for the project, Nadine pointed out that her best friend in junior high school was part of the SHARP program, and she had also known one of its directors, Ms. Sweetwine, for 10 years. "Now that I am older," Nadine wrote, "I would like to know more about this program."

Having a personal investment in her research gave Nadine a positive start to her project. From the onset and throughout the project, Nadine "behaved" like a researcher. The entries from her research log reflected the time and energy she put into the project. Following are excerpts from her log:

> 2-21-96
> There are questions that need to be answered in order for me to understand what SHARP is all about: When was the program established? Who established the program? Why? Who funds it? What does SHARP stand for? What are the advantages and disadvantages of the program?
>
> 2-26-96
> We made a circle (in class); everyone spoke about where they are, and what problems they were facing. I came to realize that most of the class was facing some kind of difficulty. Talking about it helped me to be more relaxed.
>
> 2-28-96
> Ms. Sweetwine still did not call. Tonight I will call my friend and ask him to write a note and give it to his sister to give to Ms. Sweetwine. I hope that this will work. This is my last chance.

In the first draft of her narrative, Nadine discussed the SHARP program—its goals, activities, problems, and possibilities. She began:

> SHARP is an organization that came about in the early eighties. It was established because there was an awareness that children of working parents of St. Albans were left unattended after school hours. Because of this, some got injured while others were 'getting into trouble.' SHARP provides students with a place to stay, help with their homework, food, and activities that they enjoy. Such activi-

ties are arts and crafts, playing in the gym, and on Fridays they watch 'screened' movies.

Although Nadine's instructor was pleased with her draft, she felt more details were needed. The instructor wrote:

> [Nadine], you have done a fine job. . . . While it reads well, I sense that something is missing . . . somehow I don't get a real 'feel' for SHARP or Ms. Sweetwine. What could you do to bring your readers closer in to the 'feel' of things—try playing with some detailed description of the place, of <u>her</u>. See what comes up.

Nadine responded well to her instructor's comments. Her subsequent drafts gave a better "feel" for SHARP through use of detail and quotations from Ms. Sweetwine. By the final draft, Nadine was able to place SHARP in a larger social context, successfully integrating primary and secondary sources. Following are excerpts from the final draft:

In the world today, some things are very different compared to decades ago. In the past, most men worked while most women remained at home with the children. Now within most nuclear families both parents work outside the home. Cost of living and the need for
5 independence could be the cause of this....

While children are in school, the parents are at work. Between 2 p.m. and 3 p.m. children are dismissed from school and parents are still at work. As a result, children are left alone at home. These children are known as latchkey children. Sometimes they are left with other
10 siblings and with care givers who sometimes abuse them....
Parents desperately need a safe atmosphere for their children during after school hours because these days a lot of danger lurks out there, and children are susceptible. After school programs exist in some community, but there are not enough of them. The number of
15 children out weighs the number of programs; therefore more programs need to be established because there is a growing need for them. Both parents and children benefit from such programs. I say this because the information I got from sources and Ms. Sarah Sweetwine who works at Safe Harbor After School Recreational Program (SHARP) proves this.

20 Parents are very pleased with SHARP, because it has an environment suitable for their children. Apart from that they receive help with their

homework. This seems to be the most important part of the program to all parents. Parents take whatever action necessary to try to get their children into the program '...they go to the principal, they go to the
25   District Office and they confront the teacher in charge.' (Sweetwine) It is obvious that parents like SHARP.
Over the years, much emphasis have been put on the need for good after school programs like SHARP. Studies have showed that children of working parents need these programs. The number of children left
30   unsupervised after school is increasing because some parents cannot afford to pay for child care also today, there are more single parents. 'Home Alone,' an article in *The Washington Post*, gives reason for this:

> Child abandonment, willing or unwilling, for hours or for days, is increasing in this country. It's most often the result of poverty, single parenthood, two-wage earner families and round-the-clock job shifts. (A18).

This final draft of Nadine's research paper shows a gradual increase in the ratio of lexical density. The first 200 running words ending in line 19 have a lexical density of L: 96; G: 104 (48%); the next 200 words ending in line 35 have a lexical density of L: 105; G: 95 (52%). One reason for this increase might be the inclusion of a quotation from a *Washington Post* article that is fairly high in lexical density: L: 21; G: 13 (62%) in the latter half of the excerpt.

The overall lexical density of 400 words is L: 201; G: 199 (50%) whereas the type/token ratio is 184/400 or .46. It is interesting to note that although Myrna and Nadine have the identical type/token ratio, Nadine's ratio of lexical density is 14 percent higher than Myrna's. This might suggest that Nadine tends to use a wider range of lexical items than Myrna.

The excerpt also shows certain features of formal academic writing: use of prepositional phrases of time such as "[i]n the world today" (line 1), "[i]n the past" (line 2), "[o]ver the years" (line 27); transitional phrases, for example, "[a]s a result" (line 8) and "[a]part from that" (line 21). Nadine continues to show an ability to elaborate on a topic sentence. Once she establishes that "some things are very different compared to decades ago" (lines 1-2), she immediately explains the differences in the following sentences: "In the past, most men worked while most women remained at home" (lines 2-3); "Now . . . both parents work outside the home" (lines 3-4). She also gives one possible reason for this change in working practice: "Cost of living and the need for independence" (lines 4-5).

In the second paragraph, we are told that one of the consequences of parents' being at work is that children are often left alone with other siblings or caregivers—situations that might be unsafe or even lead to child abuse. Having stated the problem, Nadine sets the stage for a possible solution—the need for a safe atmosphere for children after school; hence, the need for good after school programs. Nadine thus created the context for her research on SHARP. She asserts that both parents and children benefit from after school programs such as SHARP and she supports her claim by incorporating excerpts from her interview with Ms. Sweetwine, one of the employees of SHARP. Nadine integrates the quotation from Ms. Sweetwine effectively in lines 24-25 to show that parents would take any action necessary to get their children into SHARP.

Finally, she reinforces the need for after school programs by citing studies that have been done in this regard. We learn that the "number of children left unsupervised after school is increasing" (lines 29-30). *The Washington Post* article gives a number of reasons for this phenomenon including "single parenthood" (lines 34-35) and "two-wage earner families" (line 35).

This excerpt from her research paper shows that Nadine has clearly internalized some of the conventions of essayist writing, especially the elaboration of ideas as part of verbal explicitness and the support of claims by reference to primary and secondary sources in research. A morphosyntactic analysis of this excerpt is summarized in Table 4.

Table 4. Morphosyntactic Features. Total Number of Morphosyntactic Errors in 400 Words of Nadine's Research Paper.

	Actual Occurrences	Possible Occurrences
Verb-Related Features		
Zero inflection for:		
third person singular	1	10
past tense	0	3
verb particles	1	10
Plurals		
Zero inflection for:		
plural determiner	1	14
generic count nouns	2	25
Total:	5	62

Like Charles and Myrna, Nadine also made errors in verb-related areas, as indicated in Table 4. Overall, the error percentage for these selected features in her research paper was rather low (only about 8%), given that none of her writing appeared to be plagiarized. Although past-tense errors did not show up in her research paper, I found instances of these in other samples of her writing. Table 4 also reveals Nadine's errors with respect to plurals—a phenomenon that was common among all the participants. The following examples of error were taken from a qualitative analysis of Nadine's writing:

Zero Inflection: Verb-Related Features and Plurals

1. Blake carried guns and threaten* other.
2. He realize* that his life could have been like Blake.
3. I didn't think that it look* provocative.

Subject/verb concord

1. In some novels, the kitchen serve* as a symbol.
2. This memory establish* a moment of being for Cofer.
3. As for the rest of the family, I think Brent do* not want to be part of their lives.

Participles

1. They hadn't bother* to discuss how Anne would be spelled.
2. Maybe the cherries are suppose* to look fake.
3. Students are place* into groups according to the grade they are in.

In terms of plurals, Nadine tends to omit the -s inflection when there is what I refer to as a *singular distractor* in the sentence:

1. One of his responsibility* was to take Brent to the doctor. (One is singular and distracts from responsibilities which should be plural.)
2. Whenever her mother worked late, she was sent to one of their house*.

Like Myrna, Nadine sometimes omits the -s on certain generic count nouns:

1. The children picked mangoes, banana*, plum* and apples.
2. Her cousins are following in the footstep* of their uncle.

3. This ad deliberately appeals to minority*, offering them a sad fantasy of equality.

Overgeneralization

Many of Nadine's morphosyntactic errors related to the overuse of third person singular s. The error seemed to occur in syntactic environments where a plural subject was followed by a modifying prepositional phrase which ended with a singular noun positioned next to the verb. The modifying prepositional phrase became a distraction from the real subject:

1. Travails of <u>immigrant life</u> makes* the mind stronger. (<u>Travails</u>, the subject, is distracted by <u>life</u>, which is singular, inducing the third person <u>s</u> inflection on the verb.)
2. The males <u>in the Boatwright family</u> fits* the stereotype.
3. The essays <u>in the class anthology</u> says* a lot about identity.

There was no evidence of phonological interference with respect to spelling, or omission of the copula. There was also no evidence of Creole English usage of standard English grammatical words. This is consistent with Nadine's being less influenced by Creole English speech because of her longer residence in the United States compared to the other participants.

FINAL REFLECTIONS

Nadine had a good sense of her own language and the contradictions that inhere in the use of her home language. For example, she could recognize the irony of Creole English being denounced *in Creole English* by the very people who speak it. Such was the case with her mother and her guardian. Nadine was also aware of the fact that the strong Jamaican presence in her high school reinforced her use of the vernacular. Although her accent was less pronounced at the time of this study, she continued to be conscious of her pronunciation in English class.

Over the course of four semesters in the LIU writing program, Nadine felt her writing improved. Interestingly, the first area she pointed to as a measure of her improvement was subject-verb agreement. She said, "You know like 'the girls wal<u>k</u>' and 'a girl walk<u>s</u>' . . . yeah, I got that together now. . . . I think I got better—much, much better." That Nadine pointed to her mastering the third person <u>s</u> inflection as an indication of her writing improvement was no surprise. She was merely mirroring the preoccupation with inflections, often induced and reinforced by English teachers, to which I alluded earlier as part of our Western linguistic tradition.

Commenting on the areas in her writing that she felt had most changed, she remarked, "My introductions and transitions from one paragraph to the other . . . 'cause before I would just start an essay . . . and I used to have problems with that in high school . . . introductions and conclusions." In terms of what still needed to be improved she said, "Huh . . . just making sentences clearer to the reader, because I know what I'm talking about, but *they* don't. . . . Yeah, that's it, I think." Her comments reflected a realization on her part that essayist writing demands, among other things, cohesion and verbal explicitness. Nevertheless, she passed English 17 and moved on to sophomore literature. Finally, a comment on her writing in general: "I'm enjoying it more. Before I thought it was just a bore, but now I like putting down my words."

8

Oscar Evans

> In Jamaica, once you're in the classroom, you have to adjust your speech pattern . . . so you've been doing that for so many years, it's not purely English all the time, but you try to be as standard. . . . I mean where people can understand you.

Oscar Evans, 22, was born and raised in Kingston, Jamaica, where his immediate family still resides. He is the eldest of four children and was raised in a lower-middle-class family. His father worked at an accounting firm for several years before leaving to start his own pest control business. His mother worked as a caterer. Oscar is a serious, articulate, and confident student who is proud of his family and Jamaican heritage. He noted that although his parents did not have the opportunity to go to college, they instilled in him the importance of school:

> The funny thing about it. . . . I mean for the greater part my parents. . . . I guess probably they never get a chance to go very far in school. They went to secondary and they went to vocational, technical school . . . so I mean they got a little stuff you know, but they didn't get much . . . but

> they always stressed the importance of school. . . . I guess from that I picked up what I needed to do in order to get ahead in life.

Of the four participants in the study, Oscar was the only one who was not an immigrant in the strict sense of the word. He arrived in New York City on January 28, 1994, on a student visa, which meant that his immigrant status was temporary because his visa was valid only for the duration of his study. He was awarded an athletic scholarship for track and field to pursue a bachelor's degree at LIU, where he planned to major in marketing and finance. He also worked part-time for the campus newspaper. Having been raised in an urban environment in Jamaica *and* having attended a prestigious high school there, Oscar developed strong receptive and productive skills in standard English. However, since he had been living in the United States for only two years at the time of this study, his speech was still marked by a strong Jamaican accent.

EARLY LANGUAGE AND SCHOOLING EXPERIENCES

Oscar's earliest recollections of reading and writing were mostly positive. He began reading regularly at home where he grew up watching his parents and grandparents reading. The following sequence describes his early literacy experiences:

Researcher: Did you see your parents reading?
Oscar: Yeah, my parents and my gran'fadda and all o' dat, so I was always curious about what was goin' on. . . . I mean it wasn't like tryin' to learn to read to improve anything. It was just a matta of readin' to find out what was in the paper as such.

Oscar attended Mona Primary School in Kingston. He remembered being a good reader in school and added that many people, especially teachers, were surprised at how well he read. He recalled,

> I remember readin' my first piece. I mean I started readin' and like everybody was surprised that I was readin' at such a high level. I remember in my classroom . . . you know they used to use readin' books that they gave us at school. . . . The teacher was even surprised. . . . She used to call on me. . . . I was one of the best students in the class . . . was a little strange. . . . I mean it never occur to me that I was special. . . . I felt it comin' to me natural.

Oscar was also very proud of his writing and described the kinds of writing he did in primary school:

> My writin' was good. You know we started out with basic writin' like small topics . . . you know the name of the school. I remember like composition stuff . . . like it was based on the school and we had to tell the teacher about that school . . . the name of the principal and all o' dat.

In terms of prescriptive grammar he added,

> Well, as I say, they started from basics. We did this thing called <u>phonics</u>, where I mean was like you learn to pronounce words, then move from pronouncin' words to writin' to actually learnin' how to form sentences . . . and then move up gradually into the stricter nature of punctuation and all o' dat. . . . You know we were under the English system, and so I guess they were doing it under those rules.

It is worth noting that Oscar emphasized being under the English system. Although in the 1980s the Caribbean was in the midst of major changes in the education system (moving from British-based curricula and examinations to Caribbean-based ones), Oscar pointed out that two classic British grammar books, *First Aid in English* and *Student's Companion* were still being used in several Jamaican schools. Furthermore, despite the restructuring of education, many Caribbean people still perceive their education as British and pride themselves on their British education. Oscar, too, was proud of his education. He was particularly proud of his success on the Common Entrance Exam and stressed the significance of the exam:

> It's [the exam] looked at as one of the greatest firsts—a big stepping stone in your life. . . . Parents feel proud of your passing and all o' dat. . . . Because I remember I passed it on my first attempt and I got to attend one of the top academic schools.

HIGH SCHOOL IN JAMAICA

In 1985, at age 11, Oscar started attending Campion College, located in Kingston—a secondary school that he remarked only admitted those who scored in the top 10 percent on the Common Entrance Exam. Because the school was ranked among the best in the country, it emphasized that students speak "proper English" in order to maintain the school's reputation. Oscar stressed that at Campion students were required to speak standard English in the classroom. He said that in informal speech the teacher would not correct you, "but," he added, "if it were a case we were like readin" and we make mistakes pronouncin' the words and all o' dat, we were definitely corrected."

Oscar felt that his dialect did not affect his writing. In fact, he felt that was true for most of his high school peers. However, he pointed out that many students had difficulty trying to speak what he called "straight English":

> I didn't think that the dialect interfered with our writing in the classes because most of us spoke English. Most people doesn't have a problem writing English. The problem comes in when it's like tryin' to speak straight English like I'm speaking to you now. I'm tryin' to speak straight English . . . you'll definitely hear moments . . . you'll definitely hear 'cuts' when I'm not all that fluent.

Oscar made a curious distinction between speaking "English" and speaking "straight English." Despite his claim that most people spoke "English," he suggested that it was not necessarily "straight" (i.e., standard), and that it took some effort to speak the standard for a sustained period without any slips (Oscar calls them "cuts"). Two points may be inferred from his remarks:

1. Oscar was aware of the difference between his own English and standard English.
2. The "English" label given to the language spoken by most Caribbean people is called into question in formal situations such as interviews.

School is, of course, one such formal situation, and although language attitudes are slowly changing, success in school is still premised, among other things, on the mastery of standard English.

Oscar pointed out that at the high school level, students moved beyond "the basics." Reading and writing assignments encompassed both British and Caribbean literature. When asked to comment on his writing in high school, Oscar distinguished between language and literature. He said,

> Actually I didn't think I had a problem just writin' papers in the language sense. When I sense I had a problem was in the literature

> section of English. . . . Was like doin' a few papers for my teachers and they would make comments . . . so I was like what did she really want. . . . You know just writin' an essay on a particular topic I could just write, but when she would ask us to base a question from the book and we went to answer that question with reference to the book and all o' dat, dat's where I sometimes fall into trap.

It appears that Oscar used "language" to mean observing the rules of standard English grammar or writing "correctly." He saw writing about literature, however, as something beyond "language" (at least as he seemed to define it). Based on *his* definition of language, he was right. Writing about literature requires an engagement with language beyond syntactic correctness. In such contexts, language must be used for a range of rhetorical purposes—to inform, describe, analyze, synthesize, persuade, speculate, just to name a few.

Oscar admitted that writing analytical essays based on literary texts continued to be a challenge for him throughout high school. Nonetheless, he successfully completed high school after passing the Caribbean Examinations Council (CXC) exams. He also took and passed 'A' levels—advanced examinations in academic subjects prepared and marked in England. He left Jamaica in 1994 to pursue higher education at LIU.

WRITING AT LIU

When Oscar began classes at LIU in Spring 1994, he was surprised at being placed into English 13. After all, he went to two of the most prestigious schools in Jamaica, was awarded an athletic scholarship, and considered himself "a fairly decent writer." Still, Oscar pointed out that his English 13 instructor felt his writing was "not as in-depth as it should be" and that he didn't "elaborate enough." He then concluded that these might be the reasons why he was placed into English 13:

> Like my writin' was just off the top. . . . It wasn't as in-depth as it should be. I think that's where she [the instructor] was saying my problem was, I figured that's where my problem came. . . . Also the fact that they had this one test to go into those writin' classes. I think that's where it messed me up.

Oscar expressed some frustration at the placement test which was a one-shot exercise that demanded some amount of analysis—a task that he found rather difficult.

DISCOURSE ANALYSIS

Formal Writing

In English 13, Oscar wrote an autobiographical essay about the greatest influence on his life—sports. Following is an excerpt from the final draft of that essay:

> When I entered high school, I attempted to join the soccer team. This attempt was met by failure, as I was not selected to the team because I was unable to continue training after I friend of mine lost my training shoes which my mother had bought. She was upset with me for
> 5 carelessness, and had decided not to get me another pair. I did not let this incident deter my love and strong will to succeed in sports, and as a result, I became more focused on track and field. This sport had an advantage in that I could prove my worth as an athlete on an individual basis.
>
> 10 My involvement in sports had caused me to develop a strong personality and attitude. I had become a more disciplined student in my academic studies and an athlete with a very positive outlook on life in terms of becoming successful. Although I initially started out not making a soccer team or cricket team nor was I able to win races in my
> 15 early track and field career, the fact that I had to work hard to gain success in my choice of sport track and field made me a person able to appreciate how far I was coming from in life. Hence, I was able to recognize my achievements and use them as motivating factors in my life.

Unlike the short declarative sentences written by Myrna and Nadine in English 13, Oscar's writing shows longer sentences and more use of hypotaxis, relative clauses, and prepositional phrases. The two sentences in lines 1-4 and the long sentence in lines 13-17 provide good examples of these features. Although these sentences display the formality associated with academic essay writing, they seem markedly verbose and rather cumbersome. For example, in the sentence beginning with "[t]his attempt" (lines 1-2) and ending with "had bought" (line 4), there are two successive passive structures, "was met by" and "was not selected" (line 2); three subordinate clauses, "as I was ...," "because I was..." (line 2), and "after I [a] friend of mine" (line 3); and one relative clause that includes the past perfect tense, "which my mother had bought" (line 4). In the sentence beginning with "[a]lthough" (line 13) and ending in line 17, "initially" and "started out" (line 13) are redundant and "track and field" is repeated in lines 15-16.

There is also a subordinate clause, "nor was I able..." embedded in another, "[a]lthough I initially...career" (lines 13-14). Both sentences could have been simplified without compromising the texture of the writing.

Nonetheless, Oscar must be given credit for his attempt at approximating academic essay writing. The excerpt above is explicit and marked by clear cohesive ties (Halliday & Hasan, 1976). For example, the anaphoric references based on a demonstrative followed by a noun—"this attempt" (lines 1-2), "this incident" (line 6) and "this sport" (line 7)—are all easily recognizable. The rest of the essay traces Oscar's athletic career chronologically up until he entered LIU.

Oscar remarked that although he did well on his own autobiographical writing, he had difficulty writing essays in response to others' autobiographies. His English 13 writing instructor kept prompting him for more elaboration on such essays. Still, Oscar did well enough in English 13 to be allowed to retake the placement test to be exempted from English 14. Unfortunately, he did not pass the test. Reflecting on retaking the test, he said, "I did the test to go to 16 and they said 'no'. . . so I figured something was definitely wrong with my writing."

Oscar began English 14 with mixed feelings. On the one hand, he started to believe that something was wrong with his writing; on the other hand, he felt that his writing was above the level of the class and so he did not belong there. At any rate, he approached his writing with the same level of seriousness as he always had. For his English 14 portfolios, he only included autobiographical or creative pieces. Following is an excerpt from one essay on his image of the perfect world:

> The rules of this world make me sick. I am tired of seeing innocent as well as poor people suffer because of the poorly mismanaged resources by the so-called leaders. I have always had dreams of a perfect world. A world where I would coordinate activities to eliminate wars,
> 5 starvation, pollution, thieves, murderers, envy, hatred and greed among men. This world will be created to suit only people with a positive mind, a will, and initiative to move forward in life and to help design a plan to benefit mankind and not to contribute to his downfall.
>
> 10 My world has been created. It is that calm, tranquil masterpiece built by a generation given the divine rights by God to incorporate that unified strength of the human race. It has a refreshing atmosphere, and everyone gets along with each other. There is a strong value of morality over simple man-made laws. We do not use money to
> 15 finance wars because there is no war, and luxurious lifestyle does not exist only for one set of people because everyone lives luxuriously.

For a creative piece of writing, the language is appropriate. The short, declarative opening sentence using the simple present tense is very effective. The reader is immediately drawn into Oscar's disgust with the world as presently constituted. The idea is developed in the following sentence (lines 1-3) by a specific example of what bothers Oscar about the world. Next, he contrasts the negative image in the second sentence with a positive image of his dream of the perfect world. The rest of the first paragraph elaborates on Oscar's vision of the perfect world.

In the second paragraph, the world "has been created." By using the simple present tense throughout the paragraph, the reader is made to feel that this perfect world is real. In lines 10 and 11, Oscar uses what Allsopp (1979) calls "image-making <u>that</u>" which "brings something that the speaker [writer] is describing into the listener's [reader's] imagination as if it were actually there" (p. 103). We see that Oscar is able to use language creatively here because he is not constrained by the need to make reference to other texts. Each sentence builds on the previous one to create a cohesive text, and by extension, Oscar's picture of the perfect world. The world that has been created is described as "calm" (line 10) and built by a generation of "unified strength" (lines 11-12). Next we learn of the harmonious relationship of the people in this world: "everyone gets along with each other" (line 13) and that there is a strong sense of morality among the people.

Two instances of redundancy or perhaps even hypercorrection disrupt the flow of writing in this excerpt: "poorly mismanaged" (line 2) and "calm, tranquil" (line 10). In the case of the first, <u>poorly managed</u> or simply <u>mismanaged</u> would have sufficed. In the case of the second, one of the two words could have been eliminated.

Oscar noted that he did particularly well in English 14 (he got an 'A') because he "got to do most of [his] papers properly" as opposed to English 13 where he said, "the teacher rushed us." His success in English 14 might be partially attributed to the fact that he focused on autobiographical or nonliterary-based writing, refining only those essays for his portfolios. There were no essays in his English 14 portfolios that related to any of the texts read in class; thus, his portfolio was being evaluated on essentially one type of writing.

In English 16, it was difficult for Oscar to remain in his writing "safety zone." Almost all essay assignments required specific reference to readings done in class. An excerpt from an essay on John Edgar Wideman's *Our Time* followed by some of the instructor's comments shows Oscar's writing about literature:

This paper describes a situation where a boy named Robby found
himself being pressured indirectly by his mother and other people who
were friends of the family. This pressure came as a result of a certain
standard previously set by Robby's older brothers and sisters in their
academic achievements. Robby was expected to perform just as well as
his older brothers and sisters; however, he instead found himself
joining a gang and doing the things which he was more fascinated
with.

Robby was a member of a gang where he felt he had to be rebellious in
order to achieve a sense of pride. He got involved in this gang which
helped him to basically overcome the feeling of being left behind in his
family. He explained to his brother that growing up exposed him to a
lot of pressure, which consisted of not only peer pressure but also
pressure from his neighbours and other friends of his family to achieve
academic success like his older brother and sisters.

Robby tells John in their conversation at the prison that the fact that
John and the rest of his brothers and sisters were doing well in school,
made him become exposed to an expectation from other people to also
perform well in school (p. 224-25). He described however that he
resisted this pressure because of the genuine want of creating what
would be like a niche for himself. He visualized for himself a future
where he would be some famous actor or singer and achieve financial
success through individual talent and ability. Robby could picture
himself making a lot of money and giving back some of his rewards to
his parents so they would live a more affluent life.

Instructor's comments
Paragraph 1—Orient your reader—mention [the name of] the story and author.
Paragraph 2—Elaborate, bring in examples and quote.
Paragraph 3—This sounds like a common American dream. Why is it a problem for Robby to have this dream?

For the most part, the writing is grammatically correct, but the instructor's comments suggest that correctness is not at issue here. Oscar was being challenged to elaborate—a fundamental requirement in this type of academic essay writing. He did respond to the instructor's comments in his revision. For example, in response to the comments on paragraph 3, he added a new paragraph that began as follows:

> The dream of becoming rich by Robby, however, developed into a problem for him because the path he chose to achieve this goal would conflict with what society would accept as the proper method of satisfying his want.

The final draft of the essay turned out to be a more developed piece of writing, although it should be noted that revisions appeared to be only at points where the instructor made comments. The rest of the essay remained intact. Oscar himself admitted in his cover letter that he judged improvement based on his instructor's comments. He said, "The revision process in groups helped a little bit, but I judged my essay's improvement based mostly on what was specified by the teacher. This was because I wanted to be as accurately as possible."

Self-Assessment: Portfolio Cover Letter

In his English 16 midterm portfolio cover letter, Oscar discussed his writing process. He began as follows:

> I did not expect to face some of the difficulties which I came upon in the writing of these papers. The first paper which I found the most difficult was the final essay with drafts. This paper demanded a lot of time for me although we were supposed to free write on our various
> 5   thesis before actually starting the paper. The fact that I had to make several references to the text to support my points and related thesis took some amount of thought and preparation before I could actually transfer the information on paper.
>
> I realized that despite the group exercises which we carried out in class
> 10 to check for possible errors, I still spent a lot of time trying to put together the essay. The second most difficult paper was the in-class essay which I tried keeping the topic in focus, in order to produce a good essay. This essay however was less demanding because I was able to keep the question asked in focus.

The excerpt shows Oscar's coming to terms with the fact that essay writing takes time, especially writing with reference to other texts. Because Oscar seemed to avoid writing about literature in English 13 and 14, he did not have sufficient practice with this process; hence, the difficulty he encountered in English 16. He admitted in lines 9-11 that despite the group exercises checking for possible errors, he still spent a lot of time on the essay. The implication here, as stated earlier, is that grammatical correctness is not enough to meet the demands of academic writing.

The comments by Oscar's instructor on the abovementioned cover letter suggest that the letter itself needs development. The instructor notes, "You say you spent a long time revising in addition to these exercises, but a real description of the process itself is virtually absent (as an integrated whole). Develop these observations for final portfolio." His final portfolio cover letter is not significantly different from the midterm letter, that is, he still emphasizes the time it takes to write the drafted essays rather than provide a detailed description of his writing process:

> I must say that this portfolio was a real challenge for me. . . . The essay with drafts, as usual, required the most preparation from me; this was because with the help of readers' comments, I had to carefully analyze and observe how each draft would be improved and as a result evolve
> 5 into the final draft of the essay.
>
> The essay without drafts was not as demanding but still required the same process as the essay with drafts. The overall time taken to prepare this essay along with consultations with readers, made me become aware of different approaches to improve this essay to make it more
> 10 interesting.

Although Oscar said that he "had to carefully analyze and observe how each draft would be improved" (lines 3-4), he did not say exactly what steps he took to improve them. Likewise, in line 9 of the excerpt he said that he had become aware of "different approaches" to improve his essay. Still we are not told what these approaches were. At this point, Oscar seemed to have difficulty explicating his ideas.

In-Class Writing

Oscar's in-class writing varied depending on the degree of control he had over the topic. The language was more verbally explicit if he had total control of the topic and/or did not need to make reference to other sources. When reference had to be made to a text, Oscar typically retold the story or wrote in very general terms about the topic with little analysis but with close attention to syntactic correctness. For example, in an essay on Chinua Achebe's *Things Fall Apart*, Oscar was asked to discuss the ways in which Okonkwo, the main character, is symbolic of the values of his society. He began his essay as follows:

> Okonkwo, a well known leader and fighter in the village of Umuofia, was famous among his people and other villages for his highly valued personal achievements. These included the titles he won through fighting in the various village wrestling matches.

Oscar spent most of the essay retelling what Okonkwo did rather than discussing how it reflected the value system of his society.

Research Paper

Oscar did a semester-long research project on reggae superstar, Jamaican-born Bob Marley, based on interviews with one of Marley's sons. He was very passionate about his topic, and having known Marley's son personally, he was able to gain valuable information on Marley to enhance his research. Following is an excerpt from the final draft of Oscar's research paper (see Appendix E for full text):

> Bob Marley's interest in music was reflected at an early age when he took more interest in action songs than regular classwork. He was quoted in a television interview as saying, 'The teacher say who can write, write, and who can sing, sing. So me sing.' Bob Marley was
> 5 described by his teacher and mother as a bright boy but more meditative than aggressive when it came to learning. This shows the foundation which Bob Marley possessed and perfected to bring out his career as a world famous musician and speaker for the poor and Black people of the world.
>
> 10 Through his strong effort and powerfully worded songs Marley was able to draw the attention of millions of people in the world including world famous leaders and presidents. He voiced a strong need for social change and equal power struggle which would benefit the many suffering black and economically stricken nations of the world. He was
> 15 also particularly concerned with those nations that were being suppressed and exploited by the people in control of their governments, this included his own country of Jamaica. According to Steven Marley, his father used his music to bring to light the many injustices present in the world, and the covert methods used by people
> 20 in authority to manipulate the poorer and less fortunate societies of the world.
>
> Some of Bob Marley's more famous recorded albums spoke strongly of these injustices of society or how he grew up under very poor conditions. His deeply religious beliefs were also reflected in his songs
> 25 which sometimes quoted Bible verses and how they applied to us as people in life. Bob Marley was described by Frank Owen of the <u>New York Newsday</u> paper as a 'complex problematic figure in society.' He became fabulously wealthy leaving from his career a large sum of $35 million for his children at the end of his life. He nevertheless lived a

30   simple life observing the strict laws of his Rastafarian faith. He was also
    described by Owen as a gentleman who was a 'reformed rudeboy' and
    who knew how to take care of himself in a fight.

    Bob Marley was a revolutionary agitator who became a role model for
    Black activists everywhere, people tried to control him throughout his
35 life especially in his early days of forming his musical career. This
    however only helped him to become more vocal in his cry for social
    change worldwide.

 The ratio of lexical density in the first 200 words ending in line 19 above is L: 103; G: 97 (52%). In the next 200 words ending in line 37, there is an 8 percent increase in lexical density: L: 120; G: 80 (60%). Unlike Charles' and Myrna's research papers in which increased lexical density might be attributed to plagiarism, Oscar's lexical density appears to be related to his frequent use of adjective and adverbs: "powerfully worded" (line 10), "strong need" (line 12), "economically stricken" (line 14), "deeply religious" (line 24), "fabulously wealthy" (line 28), "strict laws" (line 30) and "revolutionary agitator" (line 33).The overall lexical density in 400 words is L: 223; G: 177 (56%) and the type/token ratio is 204/400 or .51. Oscar's writing shows the highest type/token ratio of the four participants, suggesting it exhibits the widest lexical range among them.

 It must be pointed out, though, that because Oscar seems to avoid the use of secondary sources (his only secondary reference is to Frank Owen—lines 26-27 and 28-29), one has no way of knowing how he would have handled the integration of such sources into his paper. The avoidance of secondary sources is a major omission on Oscar's part given that one of the principal requirements of research papers at LIU is to integrate primary and secondary sources. His paper thus becomes entirely "oral history."

 Still, Oscar's report of Marley's son's narrative was not vivid in its orality. For example, he did not include any direct quotations from Marley's son in his paper. The writing was all done as reported speech, which created a certain distance. The only time Marley's son was brought into the text was in lines 17-19: "[a]ccording to Steven Marley, his father...the world." Even here, Oscar paraphrased Steven's words.

 Oscar seemed to have a preference for the passive voice, which also gave his writing a feeling of "detachment" (Chafe & Danielewicz, 1987): "Marley's interest in music was reflected..." (line 1), "[h]e was quoted..." (lines 2-3), "[h]e was particularly concerned..." (lines 14-15) and "Bob Marley was described..." (line 26). Furthermore, most of the verbs in the excerpt were not action verbs, making the language feel less oral.

Nevertheless, the excerpt paints a vivid picture of Marley through Oscar's use of detail. In the first paragraph, he described Marley's early interest in music and his teacher's characterization of him. Although Marley was a well-known artist, Oscar made no assumption of the reader's knowledge. Instead, he carefully provided the details of Marley's life, both chronologically and philosophically. Each paragraph elaborates on a different facet of Marley' s life. We learn of Marley the artist/lyricist (lines 10-12), the agent for social change (lines 12-13), the spokesman against poverty and injustice (lines 17-21), the believer in religion (line 24), and finally, the revolutionary agitator (line 33).

Because Oscar's research paper was based essentially on a primary source, his success in doing research can be fairly measured only in this area. He showed some knowledge of the chronological order of narratives by charting Marley's life from his early days at school to his career as a black activist. He was able to integrate the narrative into his paper, albeit in a passive form. His use of passive rather than active verbs suggests an awareness of the passive voice being associated with a written essayist register. Finally, by developing a different facet of Marley's life in each paragraph, he seemed to have learned that paragraphs are used to elaborate on a topic. A morphosyntactic analysis of this excerpt is summarized in Table 5.

The virtual absence of morphosyntactic error in Oscar's research paper, as indicated in Table 5, reinforces the fact that his perception of writing was largely concerned with correctness. Because Oscar had many years of exposure to standard English, both in and out of school, he was very attentive to grammatical rules and their correct application, especially with regard to inflections. A qualitative analysis of his writing revealed few errors with inflections but rather a more general problem of hypercorrection. The following are examples of his writing:

Table 5. Morphosyntactic Features. Total Number of Morphosyntactic Errors in 400 Words of Oscar's Research Paper.

	Actual Occurrences	Possible Occurrences
Plurals		
Zero inflection for:		
generic count nouns	1	18
Total:	1	18

Zero Inflection: Verb-Related Features and Plurals

Unlike the other three participants, there were far fewer instances of zero inflection for verb-related features in his writing. Only in three instances—all in compound verb phrases—was zero inflection found.

1. I realized they were in a situation where they had not make* enough use of some of the facilities designed to help them make key decisions in life.
2. The school year has just began*, and it is your first day of the semester.
3. An assassination attempt was made on his life a few minutes before he was schedule* to perform at a peace concert.

There were, however, several instances of zero inflection for plurals both after determiners that modify plural nouns and in the case of generic count nouns.

1. I would not have these path* made out for me like I had in high school.
2. I have learned a lot in terms of discovering some of my strength* and weaknesses in writing.
3. Luxurious lifestyle* does not exist only for one set of people because everyone lives luxuriously.

There was no evidence of missing copula or zero inflection for possessives.

Overgeneralization

Because Oscar was very conscious of rules, especially as regards inflections, he tended to overgeneralize them, resulting in cases of hypercorrection.

1. My hard efforts in sports began to give me positive feedbacks* when I started to win medals and trophies in high school.
2. I started school with my only focus being on academics* subjects.

In the examples above, Oscar appeared to be overgeneralizing the rule of agreement. In other words a plural subject, <u>efforts</u>, must produce a plural result, <u>feedbacks</u>. By the same token, the plural noun <u>subjects</u> carries the plural modifier, <u>academics</u>.

114   CHAPTER EIGHT

   3. Whether this was coincidental or not, this made people started*
      to view Bob Marley not only as an entertainer, but also as a
      prophet.

In example 3, the past tense <u>made</u> induces the following past tense, <u>started</u>.

Sentence Structure

Oscar typically wrote long, complex sentences with many prepositional phrases or relative clauses. Some appear to be convoluted and even hyperliterate:

   1. With strong encouragement from my well-loved coach and friends, and last but not least, from my well-loved parents and relatives, who despite their negative responses shown to me as a result of my many hours spent away from home in practice, were now thankful.
   2. I therefore was not able to diverge from the idea which I was trying to bring across in this writing, in order to relate it to other issues in everyday life without carefully analysing how I would actually do this.
   3. This external source may be in the form of a group of people, who may have opinions towards a subject or issue in life, contrary to those believed in by this person.

FINAL REFLECTIONS

Oscar was adequately schooled so that he was fully aware of the differences between casual speech and genres of essayist literacy, and the appropriate use of language in various contexts. In fact, he was so concerned with using what he perceived as the "proper" or "literate" register in school, that his writing was markedly hypercorrect. This type of hypercorrection is fairly common among some natives of former British colonies. I suspect it is an overextended attempt to distance oneself from the use of Creole English (thought to be a sign of poor schooling) and to show one's knowledge of standard English (an indication of having been formally schooled).

   In terms of spoken language, Oscar admitted that in New York City he speaks the "Jamaican dialect" when he is around other Jamaicans or in informal situations, but switches to standard English once he is in the classroom or in a formal setting:

Oscar:	Yep, that's [Jamaican dialect] just about most of what I speak everyday because most of the time I'm around Jamaicans. Even when I'm not around Jamaicans, I jus' speak like that. Once I'm in a comfortable environment, I will go into it.
Researcher:	How do you make the transition when you come into the class room?
Oscar:	Actually, I do . . . because I'm used to doin' it from back home. I mean in Jamaica once you're in the classroom, you have to like adjust your speaking pattern . . . so you been doing that for so many years, it's not purely English all the time, but you try to be as standard. . . . I mean where people can understand you.
Researcher:	So you just get used to making that adjustment?
Oscar:	Yeah . . . once you're in a formal setting you adjust your speech pattern.

Because of his prolonged exposure to standard English through formal schooling, Oscar did not need to rely on an oral base and was better able to approximate academic discourse. When asked to compare the writing he did in school in Jamaica with his writing at LIU, he pointed to one significant difference:

Oscar:	Well the type of essays we got [in Jamaica] were directly related to like books, like Shakespeare books . . . was more like you had to get to the point and probably explain what something is, as opposed to say writin' a general thing from your thoughts. So you more had to focus on what was given to you . . . so you didn't really get a chance to see what your *true* writing was . . . but here you got more o' dat.
Researcher:	So you didn't have that creative space to write?
Oscar:	Right, but here you got more o' dat. So I guess you get to see what your writing is more like . . . definitely here you get to develop your own writing style.

Reflecting on his writing at LIU, Oscar believed it improved over the four semesters in the writing program although not "100 percent." He maintained, though, that although he did "learn a few things" in English 13 and 14, he did not feel he needed those courses. He reflected on his placement as follows:

> Up to now I still don't see all that big difference in what was I missing that much that I needed to be in 13. I think I could have definitely handled 16 . . . because also the feedback. . . . I mean I've shown people my paper and they were sayin' what are you doin' in 13?

Still, he identified specific areas of improvement:

> I found that I've been able to locate errors or things that never seemed obvious to me when I was writin' in 13. I've been taught how to look at things like certain aspects of my writin' on a deeper level. I've been able to expand on things that I used to give skimpish details. I've been taught how to analyze and bring out more meaning.

He also noted that there were some "finer points" that could be improved in his writing. As he said, "probably just structuring my sentences so that they wouldn't really sound too wordy." Oscar still feels that he writes best when he just gives his personal views, and he is still somewhat challenged by analyzing a specific issue from a text. Like Nadine, he passed English 17 and moved on to sophomore literature. Finally, when asked if he still read a lot, he responded, "Yeah, mostly periodicals and stuff because reading books. . . . I don't have a lot of time . . . so it's more magazines and newspapers 'cause I have to be quick. I'm busy these days."

9

Discussion and Conclusions

This study began by placing the language issues of anglophone Caribbean students in North American classrooms in a larger context. The language that these students bring to our classrooms emanates from the interplay of a host of historical, sociocultural, economic, and educational factors, which have a direct bearing on their acquisition of school-based language and discourse. The preceding narratives reflect only a part of the range of anglophone Caribbean students that writing instructors might encounter in their classrooms; taken together, however, their stories tell a great deal about the legacy of British colonization in the Caribbean, especially in terms of language attitudes, language and social identity, and language and education. The narratives also reveal what happens when students who bring that legacy must find new ways to negotiate language in the classroom.

STYLE SHIFTING

By asking the participants to reflect on their own speech patterns, I was able to elicit from them the extent to which they were acutely aware of their own style shifting both in and out of school. They knew only too well that nonstandard speech is not favored in the classroom or in other formal domains, so they tried, with varying degrees of success, to make the adjustment towards standard English in such contexts. Nadine talked of paying attention to her initial aitches, lest her "Jamaicanness" or "outsiderness" become obvious, and Oscar mentioned that he was trained in Jamaica to switch to standard English in the classroom "where people can understand you."

It is important to point out that style shifting is not always in the direction of the standard. Just as standard English is considered appropriate in formal contexts, the vernacular is appropriate and preferred in informal domains or in situations where members of the participant's linguistic group are present in large numbers. Charles mentioned that everyone in his village spoke "Creolese." Oscar, who was quite proficient in standard English, admitted to speaking the "Jamaican dialect" when he was around other Jamaicans or in a "comfortable environment." Myrna said she "[goes] off into Guyanese" if there are other Guyanese around (sometimes even in class). As mentioned in Chapter 2, Le Page and Tabouret-Keller (1985) would characterize Myrna's style shifting as an act of identity. In a similar vein, Giles, Coupland and Coupland (1991) explain this kind of style shifting in terms of accommodation theory where attitudinal factors related to feelings of solidarity or difference encourage individuals to modify their speech in the direction of the superior social reference group by use of prestige variants (*convergent accommodation*) or by use of socially marked features to emphasize a distinctive social identity (*divergent accommodation*).

SPEECH AND WRITING

The ability to switch to standard English both in speech and writing varied among the participants and depended on a number of factors. Rural residence in Guyana was clearly a factor in Myrna's and Charles' speech, which exhibited the most Creole English features. Despite Myrna's urban schooling, her speech still exhibited Creole English features, especially the dropping of initial "h" which transferred into her writing in standard English (e.g., as for has). Myrna's writing also showed the highest frequency of overgeneralization of standard English rules, suggesting a conscious effort on her part to master standard English and at the same time eliminate any trace of her vernacular in writing.

Charles' rural residence was coupled with his inadequate schooling (he went to school as little as one day a week) in a vocational institution with poor facilities. He had very little opportunity to read or write anything.

Because proficiency in standard English is acquired primarily through formal schooling, Charles was at a distinct disadvantage. This is reflected in the difficulty he had in passing his writing courses at LIU. Yet, ironically, Charles was the only participant who felt he had "no problem" with English. Perhaps his inadequate schooling prevented his recognizing the difference between his vernacular and school-based English.

Nadine, on the other hand, was raised in an urban environment in Jamaica and was forbidden to speak the vernacular by her mother and her guardian. Also, she migrated to New York City at age nine, which meant that she was exposed to a larger number of standard English speakers at an early age. Further, she continued her formal schooling in New York City with the advantage of being placed into an accelerated program for promising students in high school. All of the preceding factors helped to facilitate her proficiency in standard spoken English, and though her writing is still in flux, she is steadily developing proficiency in standard written English.

Oscar, too, was raised in an urban environment in Jamaica where there was more likely to be acrolectal speakers. In addition, he grew up watching his parents and grandparents reading, so he was apprenticed at an early age to the print code and to the habit of reading. He also attended prestigious schools in Jamaica where use of standard English in speech and writing was reinforced. Oscar's schooling in English was so focused on prescriptive grammar that we see a constant preoccupation with syntactic correctness in his writing.

DISCOURSE FEATURES IN THE PARTICIPANTS' WRITING

Informal Writing

The study showed that certain discourse features emerged in relation to the genre or type of writing assignment. When participants wrote informally, whether in journals or research logs, their writing exhibited more features of casual speech. This might suggest that the participants reverted to their vernacular patterns when they were not focused on correctness or concerned with the teacher's comments. Such informal writing, where little attention is paid to correctness, should be encouraged from time to time so that students become comfortable with writing.

Charles' dialogue between Roger and his parents used many Creole English features appropriately. Nadine's writings in her journal and research log sounded almost like conversations with herself. She questioned, observed, and even vented her frustration on the page, paying little attention to form. Myrna, too, used idiomatic expressions more typical of casual speech in her journals, as in the use of "into it" in the following sentence which begins in a rather formal tone: "I find reading mystery/suspense novel very pleasurable. . . . When I'm reading these type of book, my mind, body and soul is <u>into it</u>." In these examples, the participants demonstrated their communicative competence drawing on both modes of "orality" and "literacy" in overlapping ways (Farr, 1993).

Formal Writing

It was found that when the participants began the writing program in English 13 their written language tended to be comprised of short, declarative sentences with little or no use of hypotaxis and few subordinate clauses. There was hardly any elaboration of ideas, and their writing showed a high frequency of verbs of action. These features might be attributed to the fact that most of the writing in English 13, and to a lesser extent 14, was autobiographical or narrative, which lent itself more to features of a nonessayist oral style, especially the frequency of action verbs.

The participants often did well on autobiographical writing. Recall Nadine's story about the departure of her mother. She effectively used narrative devices of suspense and play on emotions to create a powerful story. Myrna's writing was also effective in her spelling bee story. Her use of detail and verbs of action created an appropriate atmosphere, drawing her reader into the tension of the moment.

Once the participants moved on to English 16, writing assignments were predominantly expository. They were expected not only to learn the rudiments of argumentation, analysis, synthesis, and illustration, but to demonstrate such knowledge in their essay writing. The participants seemed to think of expository writing in formal terms, and so there was an attempt on their part to be more "standard" in their grammar. The result was a general pattern of what I have called *academic interlanguage* as the participants grappled with the conventions of academic writing. Their writing exhibited at once features of casual speech and essayist writing.

There continued to be a lack of verbal explicitness, where participants seemed to assume the reader shared their knowledge or opinion on a given subject. This assumption is usually acceptable in a casual speech but not in essayist writing. Charles and Myrna tended to fall back on the phrases of common wisdom in the absence of analysis. Myrna frequently used rhetorical questions—a device that seems to be more appropriate and effective in speech than in writing. In terms of written discourse features, there appeared to be a preoccupation with morphosyntactic correctness that often led to overgeneralization of standard English rules or, in Oscar's case, very wordy sentences. Oscar's wordiness showed the negative effects of a preoccupation with correctness (a result of several years of such training in school), and underscores the need for a balance between the focus on correctness and fluency in writing pedagogy.

Another major concern of the participants was tailoring their writing to what they thought the instructor wanted. My discourse analysis showed the participants' struggle to follow their instructor's guidelines and how this was reflected in the organization and actual sentences of their essays. The participants frequently organized their essays to match precisely the order of the question(s) in the writing assignment. In many cases they even used some of the instructor's words. Recall Nadine's use of "matriarchal hegemony" or Myrna's metatext on her research paper, "as a researcher, thinker, reader and writer . . . etc." Oscar admitted that his revision was primarily guided by his instructor's (and not his peers') comments; thus the writing in his final drafts was heavily influenced by the instructor's comments. Sometimes instructor-influenced language can have iatrogenic effects. When Nadine tried to put her immigrant experience in a larger social context as required by the instructor, her writing became less effective. The incorporation of "the politics of marginalization" in the second half of her essay seemed at odds with the fresh, powerful narrative style of the first half.

In-class writing, which was done at all four levels of English, was the least successful for all the participants. The pressure to respond to a fairly sophisticated text in less than two hours, or in some cases less than one hour, produced very circular writing. In place of analysis, the participants often copied chunks of text from the prompt. They rarely seemed able to achieve the verbal explicitness required in essay writing under such time-pressured conditions. One strategy used by the participants to cope with in-class writing was to select one important issue from the text and to use it as a point of departure to connect with a personal experience. This strategy, referred to by Ball (1992) as "narrative interspersion" (p. 509), seemed to be fairly effective.

Portfolio cover letters are different from other kinds of letters in that their content is determined by the reader (in this case the writing instructor) instead of the writer so that they tend to be formulaic. The participants' cover letters exhibited more features of essayist writing and often followed the organizational patterns set forth by the instructor. Because one of the purposes of the portfolio cover letter was to discuss one's development as a writer, the participants attempted to display their improvement to the instructor by using rather formal language in their letters, which often resulted in a stilted style. Writing cover letters seemed to be more a ritualistic exercise than a true metatextual activity, as evidenced by the fact that there was little difference in form or substance between the participants' midterm and final portfolio cover letters.

Research papers were a challenge for all of the participants. Charles, Nadine and Myrna told me that English 17 was their first experience with research. Their unfamiliarity with the genre made writing the research paper a difficult exercise, especially for Myrna and Charles. Because the participants viewed research as the most formal of their school-based writing, they attempted to observe all of the conventions of academic writing in their papers. In Charles' case, he made inconsistent attempts to adhere to the rules of standard English syntax, spelling, and punctuation, and when he tried to incorporate secondary sources, he ended up plagiarizing excerpts from them. Myrna was also charged with plagiarism by her writing instructor. In addition, she had not successfully met the research objectives set forth by her English 17 instructor. It should be noted that the research paper is a very specific type of academic writing with its own conventions and ethics (especially concerning plagiarism). Although students may have been warned about plagiarism, their unfamiliarity with the research process makes the seriousness of this issue less real. Many students see research as essentially a regurgitation of the "expert's" words and they are unable to integrate successfully their own ideas with those of secondary sources. The result is often texts that give the appearance of having been plagiarized.

Nadine was able to successfully complete her research project by placing her oral history in a larger social context and documenting secondary sources appropriately. Oscar, on the other hand, only utilized a primary source in his research paper; thus, his ability to do research can only be partially assessed.

A comparison of the lexical density and type/token ratio in the research papers of the four participants revealed that Nadine and Oscar showed a higher ratio of lexical density compared to Myrna and Charles. This suggests that Nadine and Oscar may have begun to internalize the features of essayist writing. Although Myrna and Nadine's papers revealed the same type/token ratio, Nadine's higher lexical density suggested a wider range in vocabulary that was more in keeping with academic writing. As noted earlier, Oscar's writing showed the highest type/token ratio. Table 6 summarizes the lexical density and type/token ratio in the participants' research papers.

After four semesters in the writing program, Myrna's, Nadine's, and Oscar's writing revealed longer sentences with greater use of hypotaxis, a higher degree of verbal explicitness and more lexical density—indications that they had begun to internalize some of the salient features of academic writing. Still, these features were in flux, their use varying with the type of

Table 6. Ratio of Lexical Density and Type/Token Ratio in 400 Words of Participants' Research Papers.

Participant	Lexical Density	Type/Token Ratio
Charles	L: 149; G: 251 (37%)	177/400 or .44
Myrna	L: 144; G: 256 (36%)	184/400 or .46
Nadine	L: 201; G: 199 (50%)	184/400 or .46
Oscar	L: 223; G: 177 (56%)	204/400 or .51

writing assignment. But such fluctuation is the nature of interlanguage and the mark of a developing writer.

Charles was a special case. First of all, he provided fewer writing samples than the other participants, with the result that there was a smaller corpus from which to evaluate his writing. Secondly, it appeared that he did not revise many of his essays, which gave him less writing practice. As a result, there was very little change in his writing over the course of four semesters. His writing revealed sporadic attempts at observing standard English rules, but he ultimately failed for lack of sufficient practice. After a two-semester absence from school, he had a formidable task ahead to catch up on his writing skills.

MORPHOSYNTACTIC FEATURES

Table 7 summarizes the errors found in the participants' writing based on a general qualitative analysis as well as a quantitative analysis of 400 words in their research papers. Participants are listed only if the error was salient.

Table 7 shows that the overwhelming majority of morphosyntactic errors in the participants' writings were verb-related. This strongly suggests that the zero inflection on the verb in Creole English exerts a strong influence on the participants' written language, despite several years of formal schooling, and manifests itself in their interlanguage in the form of transfer or overgeneralization. The findings also indicate that Charles' writing exhibited errors in all six areas investigated, which suggests that he showed the strongest Creole English influence in his writing. Next is Myrna, whose writing revealed errors in three categories—verb-related features, plurals, and phonological interference on syntax. It should be noted that her writing

Table 7. Summary of Morphosyntactic Errors of All the Participants in the Six Major Categories Investigated.

1. Verb-related features

    Zero copula — Charles
    Zero inflection for:
        third person singular — Charles, Myrna, Nadine
        past tense — Charles, Myrna, Nadine
        verb participles — Charles, Myrna, Nadine, Oscar
    Overgeneralization:
        third person singular -s. — Myrna, Nadine
        past tense inflection — Myrna, Oscar
        third person plural — Myrna

2. Plurals

    Zero inflection for:
        plural determiner — Charles, Myrna, Nadine, Oscar
        generic count nouns — Charles, Myrna, Nadine, Oscar
    singular distractor — Nadine

3. Possessives

    Zero inflection on possessor — Charles

4. Phonological interference on spelling — Charles, Myrna

5. Front focusing — Charles

6. Creole English usage of standard English words — Charles

showed at once the most evidence of overgeneralization and phonological interference on spelling, suggesting a strong attempt to internalize standard English rules while still being influenced by Creole English. Nadine's and Oscar's writings only revealed errors in two areas—verbs and plurals—which means they are much further removed from Creole English influence than Myrna and Charles and are thus becoming more proficient in standard written English.

REFLECTIONS ON FOUR SEMESTERS IN THE WRITING PROGRAM

For all of the participants, the first area they mentioned in discussing improvement in their writing was their ability to be more correct syntactically and to locate grammatical errors. Myrna still had concerns about her grammar, especially subject/verb concord, and Nadine was proud that she finally understood "the girl walks." Oscar was pleased that he could finally "locate errors" in his writing. This phenomenon was not surprising, for as Shaughnessy (1977) notes, "much about the remedial situation encourages the obsession with error" (p.8).

Beyond errors or correctness, all the participants except Charles felt they had improved in other areas of their writing. Oscar believed his writing had become more analytical. Nadine liked the fact that she was able to do better introductions and conclusions. Myrna felt that she had learned how to paraphrase, summarize, and quote appropriately. Charles felt, however, that his not taking the advice of his English 13 instructor to get a tutor might have deterred his progress in writing. Still, he was the only one who felt he had no serious problems with writing.

Despite their recognizable improvement, Oscar and Myrna questioned their placement in the basic writing program. Oscar felt he was a "decent writer" and after showing his writing to friends, they wondered why he was placed in English 13. He believed that he could have done just as well had he been placed in English 16. Myrna was not only surprised at her placement in English 13 (after being in Honors English in high school), but felt that English 13 and 14 were not useful at all because they were essentially the "same process of writing."

PLACEMENT

The question of placement is an important one and merits some attention. I mentioned earlier that the placement test at LIU requires students to respond in essay form to an unknown text, usually on a sociopolitical topic, within a two-hour time frame. Students are required to show a clear understanding of the text and to analyze some of its salient points in a coherent manner. This is a formidable challenge for many first-year college students, and even those who might do well on the syntactic level often fall short on analysis. I suspect this was the case for Oscar and Myrna. Nadine admitted that such impromptu tests made her nervous and her writing suffered under the time pressure. Charles' inexperience with academic writing would clearly not have prepared him to do well on such a test. So for these various reasons, the participants were all placed in English 13.

One might question the nature of the test itself. Approximately 60 percent of incoming freshmen at LIU were placed in the basic writing program after taking the placement test. As previously stated, the placement test at LIU, as in many other universities across the United States, is a gatekeeping device, based primarily on demonstrating proficiency in essayist literacy. Farr (1993) points out the inequities in such gatekeeping practices. She argues that "not all persons have equal instructional access to the learning of essayist literacy" (p.13), particularly those who have not been socialized into this way of speaking. In this study, Charles was clearly one such person. Furthermore, access to essayist literacy cannot be assumed to translate to its internalization in the exact manner it was taught. We see that Oscar, who has had many years of formal schooling, even at prestigious schools, ended up with the same placement as Charles, who had far less formal schooling. This says less about the intelligence or language proficiency of Oscar and Charles and more about the arbitrariness of placement practices. Placement tests of the "one-shot" written essay kind are in need of serious revision. As currently administered, they do not address the range of discourse and learning styles that students bring to school nor do they take into account the pressures of the test situation. If we must have placement tests, then they should be designed to include a choice of genres, thereby giving students with varying levels and types of verbal ability the fairest chance to "perform" at their best. Also, as Farr suggests, if we are to improve students' performance in the genres of essayist literacy, we ought to provide "instructional contexts in which learners can practice the genres in appropriate and comfortable roles" and at the same time "facilitate the learning of new genres as extensions of those already known" (p. 16).

BROADER ISSUES

Differences in Writing Between Caribbean and American Schools

The participants all pointed to some fundamental differences between writing at school in their home countries and writing in New York City schools. First of all, most anglophone Caribbean schools still follow a traditional British grammar school method of teaching. Change toward alternative methods is in progress, albeit slowly. Oscar noted that two classic British grammar books were still being used in many Jamaican schools. Nadine recalled doing pattern drills like "See Sally Run." More importantly, writing was typically a one-shot exercise. Students were not expected to submit drafts to the teacher for comment. They were usually asked to respond to an essay question on their own, and it was understood that there would be an acceptable level of syntactic correctness, including correct spelling, before the writing was given to the teacher. The student's personal opinion on the subject was rarely solicited. It was more important that they "stick to the facts."

In many American schools and colleges, by contrast, and specifically at LIU, the writing process in recent years has been premised on the notion of revision and teacher/peer response. Students are encouraged to do drafts of their essays and to share these with the writing instructor and their peers. They are expected to show some analysis of the subject in their writing and at the same time to include their opinions. Focus on syntactic correctness is seen as part of the editing phase in writing. Myrna mentioned that she found the demand for analysis and elaboration challenging, as she was not used to this kind of writing in Guyana. Nadine had some exposure to the drafting process in high school in New York City so this was not entirely new to her. She mentioned to me that she liked the peer response process and looked forward to the comments on her writing from her classmates. Oscar admitted having difficulty with analytical writing even in Jamaica. He showed some improvement in this area, although he still preferred the freedom to write his own opinions. As mentioned earlier, he believes it helps you in developing "a writing style."

The participants, then, were still in the process of learning the kinds of writing that were expected of them in American institutions of higher education. They were experiencing what I described in Chapter 3 as *linguistic acculturation*. The process is slow and not without its frustrations. With the exception of Charles, I expect that they will all succeed over time. Charles' deficit in schooling coupled with his tendency to drop out makes his success in mastering essayist literacy highly unlikely in the foreseeable future.

LANGUAGE ATTITUDES

What's in a Name?

One of the most striking observations to come out of this study was the various names the participants gave to their vernacular. At different times, their home language was described as *Jamaican, Guyanese, patois, Creolese, dialect,* or *broken English.* I noted that none of the participants used the linguistic terms, Creole or Creole English, to describe their vernacular. It appeared that the participants were not familiar with the linguistic terms, and if they were, they associated them with something negative or backward.

The participants only used the various names mentioned above to refer to their language use at home or in informal domains. In school, and other public formal domains, they generally described their language as "English," and more importantly, thought of themselves in these contexts as native speakers of English. Two factors might account for this perception: (1) As mentioned in Chapters 2 and 3, the constant interaction of Creole English and standard English along the continuum has prevented Creole English from attaining autonomy as a language in its own right. Given that anglophone Caribbean natives have no other autonomous ethnic language such as Twi or Yoruba to consider their own (ethnic languages were dispensed with during slavery), they have been forced to lay claim to the colonizer's language and (2) English was imposed as the official language in British colonies, effectively rendering the mass vernacular as a subordinate, aberrant language, or even worse, a nonlanguage.

Colonization instilled the belief that standard (British) English is the native language of anyone born and raised in a former British colony. Because language is such an intimate part of social identity (McGroarty, 1996), it is not surprising that speakers of low prestige dialects would want to publicly identify themselves with the prestige dialect. Furthermore, claiming to be a native speaker of English suggests that not only does one speak a legitimate language (as opposed to an aberrant one), but also that one has membership in the anglo community, which confers a measure of high social status.

Stigmatization of Creole English

We see from the narratives that the stigmatization of Creole English is hierarchical and very much part of a stratified social order that uses language as a gatekeeping device. Both Charles and Myrna, who hail from rural areas where the basilect predominates, told of their basilectal speech being made fun of by urban residents whose speech is typically mesolectal or acrolectal. Recall that Myrna said she consciously adjusted her speech toward the more prestigious urban variety when interacting with her urban high school peers in Guyana (perhaps an attempt to mask her rural identity). On the other hand, Nadine and Oscar, who grew up in the capital city of Jamaica, found that their urban vernacular was not acceptable in school. Only the acrolect, or what Oscar calls "proper English," was allowed in school. As noted in Chapter 3, the school is perhaps the chief custodian of standard English, and despite arguments presented in favor of using students' vernaculars in school as a vehicle for acquiring standard English (Alleyne, 1994; Nichols, 1996; Rickford, 1996), there has been little tolerance for any deviation from the standard dialect in school, especially in written language. Yet despite their schooling in the Caribbean, all of the participants found that their English was marked as different once they came to New York City. Once again, they were seen as linguistic outsiders.

Creoles in the Western Linguistic Tradition

One of the most vexing problems continuing to affect Creole linguistics is the persistent negative social psychological attitudes and interpretations that have emerged in regard to Creole languages, and indeed to any suggestion of their use in schools. I would argue that two factors account for this problem. First, there is the linguistic question of the genesis of Creoles, and secondly, there is the social legacy of European colonization. Of course, the two factors are not mutually exclusive. In fact, as Alleyne (1994) notes, these negative attitudes prevail precisely because Creole language theories have been developed within a Western linguistic tradition, which definitionally links them to pidgins and often accounts for them through processes of simplification. Alleyne is correct when he argues that

> the simplification assigned to creoles is not the form sometimes inferred in the process of change from Anglo-Saxon to English or from Latin to French, but some kind of drastic, extreme, extraordinary or unnatural simplification. (p. 9)

This model on which Indo-European language families are based ignores the fundamental changes that may occur through language contact situations typical of Creole languages (the Caribbean is a prime example). Alleyne makes the point that

> it is easy to see how these ideological assumptions about natural language have come to support and fuel those social psychological attitudes that are based on the perception that these languages are corrupt, deviant derivations within the Western linguistic tradition and concomitantly on the notion of their inadequacy. (p. 9)

The ideological assumptions alluded to by Alleyne are reinforced in Caribbean societies where British colonization imposed a rigid linguistic hierarchical structure that gave British English the highest status. Therefore, although linguists such as Bickerton (1981) and Holm (1988) have linked Caribbean Creole languages to West African languages, the general population still evaluates these languages using Western linguistic norms. Alleyne

(1994) gives the example of the Western linguistic norm that emphasizes that morphological inflections are an essential part of the ideal language structure. This study is itself testimony to my own participation in that tradition, as evidenced by the preponderance of examples on morphological inflections (or lack thereof) from the participants' writings. The point is that as long as Creole languages remain within this normative tradition, they will continue to be stigmatized.

Furthermore, colonization left behind a stratified social order, which ensured that standard English as a dominant dialect would only be spoken by a minority who are likely to be at least middle class, have had uninterrupted access to formal schooling, and are urban residents. Those who find themselves outside of this minority are often seen not only as linguistically but socially disfavored, for their language is a painful reminder of an identification with lower ranking social classes from which the minority elite would rather distance themselves (recall that Charles said he was often referred to as "country man," that is, of low social class, whenever he visited the capital city).

In the United States, the situation is similar with regard to African-American Vernacular English (AAVE). As a language spoken by a socially disfavored group, it is certainly viewed negatively. The recent national controversy over Ebonics, which is simply another name for AAVE, underscores not only popular attitudes about nonstandard languages but is reflective of a social order in which race, class, and language are intertwined in complex ways.

Can these negative social psychological attitudes towards Creoles or nonstandard languages in general be changed? Not easily, and certainly not without radical change in the social order. Linguistic prejudices are not compartmentalized. They are intricately tied to other race-based and/or class-based prejudices (i.e., how we view the speakers of particular dialects). A language is only positively evaluated to the extent that its speakers are viewed favorably. We are then faced with a "catch-22" situation—a change in attitudes can only come about by changing the status quo, but the status quo can only be altered by a change in attitudes. First, in order for speakers of nonstandard languages to move beyond their marginalized status, they would need to play a more active role in governmental and institutional practices. Yet their very language prevents them from gaining access to these institutions. Second, *nonstandard* by definition means "not standard," which suggests the language is measured against a standard variety and is therefore ranked as subordinate. Third, any attempt to completely separate Creole English or AAVE from standard English would present practical difficulties, given that both languages draw the bulk of their lexicon from English. Finally, there is the question of the language communities themselves.

Morgan (1994) and McGroarty (1996) both point out that whenever attempts are made by linguists or educators to validate languages such as Creole English or AAVE, particularly to advocate their use in schools, some of the most vehement opposition comes from within the communities themselves. As McGroarty states,

> Parents who believe that they may have been stigmatized because of their language are particularly eager to have their children acquire a second language. . . . [Those] who use a community variety such as African American Vernacular English may well oppose the use of such literacy instruction even when they reveal a detailed knowledge of and loyalty to this variety. . . . It is simply assumed that the home dialect need not be taught in school which is the place for formal instruction in and practice of the standard language. (p. 20)

This sentiment is shared by most parents in Caribbean Creole English-speaking communities in the Caribbean and abroad (See Rickford [1999] for a brief discussion on the resistance of the Caribbean community to an English-language curriculum that took creole usage into account).

We see, then, that attitudinal change is an extremely complicated matter. It is part and parcel of larger social and historical forces. Although change is not completely impossible, it is slow and will certainly continue to be met with fierce resistance. It seems that any chance of a positive change in attitudes towards nonstandard language must begin in the communities themselves and be grounded in a firm political will. Only when a marginalized community collectively fights for legitimate recognition of its language (as Haitians have done with Haitian Creole) can there begin to be any wider social and political acknowledgment of the group and its language. One way to help language minority communities rectify the view that their language is inferior or oppositional to what Smitherman (1994) calls "the language of wider communication" is to implement a language policy that involves the collaboration of the community and school, one that is premised on the notion that language is a resource rather than a problem. In the following section I propose such a language policy that, I believe, best responds to the sociohistorical, educational and linguistic issues raised in this study.

A "RESOURCE-FULL" POLICY

Ruiz (1988) delineates three social orientations to language planning—"language-as-problem, language-as-right and language-as-resource" (p. 3). He argues that the first two orientations, and especially the first, have dominated the research on language planning and have been unsuccessful in enhancing the status of minority languages. A brief discussion of the first two orientations is necessary before proposing the third.

Orientation refers to a complex of dispositions toward language and its role in society. As Ruiz states,

> these dispositions may be largely unconscious and prerational because they are at the most fundamental level of arguments about language. . . . Yet, an important role of the metatheoretician of language planning is to make these orientations obvious. (p. 4)

Orientations are essential to language planning because they frame the way we talk about language and language issues. They are certainly related to language attitudes, for as Ruiz asserts, "they constitute the framework in which attitudes are formed [and] they help to delimit the range of acceptable attitudes toward language and to make certain attitudes legitimate" (p. 4). One way to discover orientations is by examining language policy.

Ruiz argues that the dominant orientation underlying language policy and pedagogy in the past has been *language-as-problem* whereby minority students' languages either had to be fixed, ignored, or eradicated altogether. This orientation has manifested itself in various forms—first, in the *deficiency model* of Bereiter and Engelmann (1966), who were suggesting that the use of nonstandard Black English was indicative of minimal intelligence or cognitive deficiency. This same thinking gave birth to the notion of compensatory education in England—an unsuccessful attempt to compensate for a supposed linguistic deficit in anglophone Caribbean children by providing separate, intense language instruction in standard English.

Second, the *assimilationist* model tries to ignore the student's home language, that is, teach standard English and the home language will disappear—a strategy that has been tried in England, Canada, the United States, and the Caribbean as mentioned earlier. The basic premise of this orientation is that the student's home language is simply a deformed version of English that will disappear with overt and systematic instruction and correction in standard English. Gilyard (1991) refers to this as the *eradicationist* strategy (p. 70). He contends that eradicationists believe that standard English is the only language variety that has a legitimate function within the school. And since "erasing [the] dialect is a worthwhile aim, the reasoning goes, the earlier such treatment is initiated the better off the speaker of that dialect will be" (p. 70). But Gilyard cautions that eradicationism is "definitely wrong" and furthermore "has never actually worked" (p. 72). Farr (1993) supports Gilyard's point by noting that although many in these "new" populations are learning to talk and write like "The Man," aspects of their own verbal styles will continue to find their way "into" essayist literacy, expediting the transformation of this dominant register. (p. 33)

This study underscores both Farr's and Gilyard's points, for we see that, despite formal schooling, the participants' Creole English continued to manifest itself in their speech and writing. As Rickford (1999) contends, "it [the students' vernacular] *will* emerge in the classroom, and how teachers respond to it can crucially affect how the students learn to read, and how well they master Standard English" (p. 338). The notion, then, that standard English is the only legitimate language variety in school is at best, idealistic. In fact, as schools continue to be a site of of contact between the standard English of essayist literacy and the growing number of nonstandard English speakers, the very definition of English itself might be called into question.

Labov (1981) also warns against the tendency to eradicate the student's home language:

> American education has always been concerned with nonstandard English, but primarily in a negative way. It has been the object to be overcome, rather than something to be studied and understood in its own right. (p. 1)

As noted in Chapter 3, assimilationist or eradicationist orientations did not improve the school performance of anglophone Caribbean students in either England or Canada, and in fact, placed the students' communities in an oppositional relationship with the school.

The language-as-right orientation presents its own problems. In this orientation, as Ruiz states, language is seen as a basic human right. Two kinds of rights are usually advocated—the right to freedom from discrimination on the basis of language and the right to use one's home language in the activities of communal life. The first right entails demanding access to formal processes like voting, civil service exams, public employment and legal and administrative proceedings by providing forms and other printed material in both English and the community language. The second includes the right to personal freedom and enjoyment—concepts that are quite difficult to define. Ruiz argues that the fundamental problem with this orientation is that

> terms included in the legal universe of discourse do not incline the general public toward a ready acceptance of the arguments. Terms like "compliance," "enforcement," "entitlement," "requirements," and "protection" create an automatic resistance to whatever one is talking about. Their use creates confrontation. (p. 13)

Furthermore, a right is not merely a "claim to" something but also a "claim *against*" someone. Thus, as Ruiz concludes,

> it becomes one group invoking rights against another—children vs. school; parents vs. school boards; majority vs. minority groups; some minority groups vs. others; state rights vs. federal authority; and so on. (p. 13)

Ultimately, the rights of different groups become difficult to reconcile.

The problems illuminated above in regard to the language-as-problem and language-as-right orientations suggest that a third orientation should be explored. Here, I endorse Ruiz' proposal for a language-as-resource orientation, but I delineate more specifically how this orientation might work vis-à-vis anglophone Caribbean communities or any other linguistic minority group such as African Americans. First, language planning efforts should start with the assumption that language is a resource to be *managed, conserved, and developed,* and should regard language minorities as important sources of expertise. This orientation serves three functions:

1. It brings the community into a collaborative relationship with the school.
2. It can enhance the status of the community language.
3. It can begin to ease tensions between language majority and language minority groups.

Although this orientation is by no means novel, it has heretofore been proposed and/or practiced on merely token levels. Typically, writing teachers are given a handbook or offered the occasional workshop that presents a limited list of features of the community language that contrast with standard English features. Teachers are then expected to simply look for, and of course correct, these features if and when they appear in students' writings. Pedagogy of this sort can be reductive or worse, counterproductive. Whereas knowledge of the features of students' home language is crucial, as has been shown in this study, it is not sufficient. Focusing solely on linguistic features without a clear contextual understanding of the broader social context in which language minorities operate gives no real space or voice to the community language as a legitimate resource in a wide range of linguistic options (McKay & Wong, 1988). I propose a list of ways in which the community and school can truly bring their "Englishes in contact" by utilizing the community language as a resource to enrich other kinds of language learning taking place in school.

Schools and colleges should:

1. Invite dialect writers, poets and storytellers from the community into English classes and/or workshops to share their work and to explain the sociocultural context in which their writing takes place. A language is best validated by the lived experience of its people.
2. Work directly with competent community members on language-related projects such as staging plays and cultural events that utilize Caribbean Creole English and/or AAVE.
3. Host regular exhibits and/or sales of books, artwork and other items produced by language minority groups. This should not be merely a function of Black History month. Such annual displays perpetuate tokenism.
4. Provide funding for ongoing faculty development on cultural and linguistic diversity.
5. Ensure that studies done by linguists on nonstandard languages be made readily available in community, school, and college libraries.
6. Encourage community members to become active on school boards to help shape and implement language policy.

Teacher Preparation and Language Pedagogy

I would also recommend that:

1. Teacher training programs include courses in sociolinguistics that address language diversity and writing instruction. Such courses should familiarize teachers with the linguistic features of community languages as well as sensitize them to the history, culture, teaching, and learning styles of language minority groups.
2. In English classes students:
    (a) read, write and share stories in their home language and standard English. Students from the community can be used as experts on interpreting linguistic items and providing the cultural context for such texts.
    (b) Read works by community members who write in both the home language and standard English. This helps students to see their home language in juxtaposition to the standard dialect rather than in opposition to it.

(c) Be encouraged to write research papers on the community language. Students can easily function as participant researchers in their own work, thereby developing their metalinguistic awareness.
3. In English classes teachers:
(a) Familiarize themselves with the linguistic, cultural, and educational backgrounds of their students. This information should be obtained through student questionnaires given at the beginning of the semester. The sooner the instructor is informed about students, the better s/he is able to respond to their needs. Although all teachers encounter students from different backgrounds in their classes, teachers in inner-city schools and colleges with sizeable percentages of culturally diverse students should make a special effort to familiarize themselves with the cultures of these students.
(b) Encourage dialogue writing (and even role play) using both the home dialect and standard English as a way of teaching language variation in different social contexts.
(c) Use the discourse patterns found in students' writings to discuss their appropriateness for various genres and audiences and to compare and contrast rhetorical styles between the home and school culture.
(d) Probe students for clarification whenever morphosyntactic or semantic features in students' writing impede communication. These instances can serve as opportunities to compare and contrast Creole English or AAVE and standard English features.
(e) Encourage honest, meaningful dialogue on language difference and language attitudes, particularly focusing on the history, range, and complexity of attitudes in regard to nonstandard languages, and their effects on education and the wider culture.

DIRECTIONS FOR FUTURE RESEARCH

The sharp increase in Caribbean and other ethnolinguistically diverse students in American colleges reflects the rapidly changing demographics of America as part of a worldwide trend of population movement. It has challenged educators to question their own assumptions about such highly charged issues as race, class, cultural diversity, immigration, standard and nonstandard language, and literacies.

This study has shown that the complex array of social factors that account for the linguistic diversity among students today has posed new challenges for the field of sociolinguistics. Cheshire (1991) notes, for example, that

> many fundamental concepts that have long been taken for granted within sociolinguistics become problematic when they are viewed from a multilingual perspective, rather from the monolingual perspective in which they were originally developed. (p. 2)

The language of anglophone Caribbean students in particular, as exemplified by this study, underscores the fact that concepts such as speech community, native/nonnative speaker, standard/nonstandard English, and indeed the very notion of English itself can no longer be easily defined. Future sociolinguistic studies should reexamine these concepts, often assumed to be self-evident, taking into account what Hymes (1980) calls "stable multilingualism" (p. 403)—an old idea in the world but one only now being forcibly acknowledged in the United States. Studies should also examine the impact of population movement and crosscultural interactions on language use. In the case of Caribbean students, research should be done on their literacy practices outside of school and on the effects of staggered migration on their school performance. Finally, a comparative study of education systems in the Caribbean and the United States would go a long way towards enhancing understanding of the language and literacy practices of Caribbean students.

Appendix A

SAMPLE PLACEMENT TEST FOLLOWED BY QUESTIONS

Read the following passage and write an essay in response to it. The passage is taken from Ella Taylor's "TV Families: Three Generations of Packaged Dreams." The essay questions will ask you to explain what you think Taylor is saying about television families.

Passage

Few contemporary forms of storytelling offer territory as fertile as television for unearthing changing public ideas about family. The tube is at once the most truly popular and the most relentlessly familiar entertainment medium we have. And our national culture is so thoroughly suffused with its images that you needn't ever have seen "The Cosby Show" or "All in the Family" or "Ozzie and Harriet" to know the outline of what these TV institutions are about. Your kids, your parents, your friends and co-workers, or failing these, other media will tell you even if you belong to that tiny group of perverse social isolates who proudly declare they don't even own a television or that they watch only "Masterpiece Theatre" and wildlife documentaries. The shared experience of tele-history has become one of the major ways in which we locate ourselves in time, place, and generation, and at the heart of that history lies television's obsession—the family.

* * *

Of course, television is no more a mirror of (or an escape from) the social world than any other fiction. True, television's naturalism feeds our expectations of verisimilitude. Its mimetic visual form persuades us that Ozzie Nelson lives on, schmoozing the day away with his neighbor across the yard; that the Bunkers really live in Queens; that the Huxtables really frolic day after day in a well-appointed Manhattan town house. But family life never resembled that of the Nelsons, the Bunkers, or the Huxtables, at least not in any narrowly sociological sense. Like all storytelling, TV speaks to our collective worries and to our yearnings to improve, redeem, or repair our individual and collective lives, to complete what is incomplete, as well as to our desire to know what's going on out there in that elusive "reality."

Questions

Now write a single essay addressing the following questions: What do you understand Taylor to be saying about TV families? What does she mean when she says that "the shared experience of tele-history has become one of the major ways in which we locate ourselves in time, place, and generation"?

Taylor is not the only expert here. Do you agree with her that "TV speaks to our collective worries and to our yearnings to improve, redeem, or repair our individual and collective lives"? Why or why not? Offer examples from your own experiences and observations.

Appendix B
Charles' Writing Sample

CONVERSATION BETWEEN ROGER AND HIS PARENTS

Roger is a son of a doctor who came from the islands to make life better for his son and wife. While Roger find it hard to cope with peer pressure at school, his father had to work two and three job just to provide a good home for him.

One day while sitting in the living room the phone ring it a girl for Roger. Mother, said to Roger, there is a girl on the phone.

Roger: Who is it?
Mother: Some girl say her name is gina and stop hiding form her.
Popa: Isn't that the girl I see you with the night in front the store?
Roger: Yes.
Popa: That was fast—it donot take you long to do something then start hiding right.

Mother:	Would both of you shut up you all are acting like babies.
Popa:	Woman, you dose not like the idea that your son is talking to a young lady.
Mother:	Talking is not the problem, but when you are doing something else, that a hole big deal.
Popa:	Then what is the problem? and please donot say nothing.
Mother:	Why don't you ask your son since you see the girl and I didn't.
Popa:	I thought you brougth the girl to see your mother boy.
Roger:	No.
Popa:	Why didn't you bring the girl to see your mother?
Roger:	You know how mother act when she see I bring somebody new in the house.
Popa:	He is right, dear, you all ways act like how long is this one is going to last for.
Mother:	Oh, that the way you all feel. ok, just remember that I was a young lady too once and that is wrong what your son's doing.
Popa:	What is that?
Mother:	Use young lady like a pecace of tools.
Popa:	I don't see it that way.
Mother:	I donot give a dawn how you see it, but you would see it went the girl reach here.
Popa:	What is she coming here with that would make you mad?
Mother:	You are acting like that son of you is so good that he would not do anything wrong, but you will be surprise for the second time.
Popa:	I know that he did not get a next girl with a kid.
Mother:	You are starting to wise up to things that he are doing then hide.
Roger:	Mother, how can you do something like that to me without telling me?
Mother:	Just like how you father meet her and I didn't that how.
Roger:	It is so unfear to do that.
Popa:	Boy, what are you afraid of? she just going to bring the kid to see her grand-parents.
Mother:	That is a good question for the first time me and you agree on something concerning your son.
Popa:	Boy, I am talking to you. what are you afraid of but that girl coming here?
Roger:	Nothing, sir.
Popa:	So why are you acting like a man who just commit the biggest crime in the world?
Roger:	I do not know, so can both of you stop looking at me like that.
Mother:	Boy, you surprise me a lot. I teach you would learn from the first time.

Popa: He dose not hear so went the girl reach here I would let she do anything to him.
Mother: Why are you looking at it that way? you alway carrying out for an order grandkid.
Popa: I thought it would have come from the same girl, not with a defferent one.
Mother: I guess he take after his father. Can stay one place too long.
Popa: I know you did not just say that to me.
Roger: Why are both of you fighting over something that is my problem?
Mother: When you start acting like you can take care of your own we will gradly stop fighting.

The door bell ring. it was gina with something in her hand. She inter juice her self to my mother.

Gina: How are you, Miss Brown?
Mother: I am fine, gina. it take me long enough to meet you, but I am glad to see you.
Gina: I always come here, but I leave early, because I work from three to ten. Roger said you come home late.
Mother: Yes, that is true, but I am still glad to see, also heard a lot about your from his father.
Gina: Yes, I met Mr. Brown, he is a nice person.

**********Roger apair*******

Roger: Hi Gina, how are you and the baby doing?
Gina: We are fine. Mr. and Mrs. Brown, I did not come here to cause no problem between parents and son.
Mother: It would not be no problem because went you call he start telling us everything about the kid and how he was deining it.
Gina: I know he was doing that so I was not looking for anything from him just for his daughter to know her father.
Mother: I donot care what you are doing, the fact remind that roger have a daughter and he have to take care of it.
Gina: That it ture, but I teach it would cause problem, but you all take me into with a warm heart.
Mother: This is my only son and I am glad that he have a other kid although he did told me earlier. but it is o.k. now he have a resonpable to take care of.
Popa: So what are you looking forward for my son to do for you and the kid?

Gina: I just wanted him to know his daughter, instead of some one strange man she call father. I just wanted him to meet his blood and love it like he love me before we had this baby.

Mother: That is honest and I hope that he would stop running around and stick with you and the little girl.

After this meeting with gina and the discussion she had with roger parent, Roger and gina settle the little augrement they have and get an apartement where they were rising the daughter.

Appendix C
Myrna's Writing Sample

UNFAIR COMPETITION IN A DISHONEST AND RACIST SOCIETY

A person's identity may be shaped by another person, a place or an incident. There is one particular incident that has shaped my understanding of this world and my life. I was about eleven years old. I was in primary school. I mentioned primary school because the school system in Guyana goes as nursery, primary, secondary and college. The board of education decided on an inter-school spelling "B" competition which also included maths, science and social studies.

      The competition was between two schools. Each school had three competitors representing. Student from each participating school would attend to cheer for their respective school. In the room where the competition was held there was a long desk and a long bench on either side where the competitors sat. There was also a buzzer which you would press if you know the answer of any question asked. The two schools which competed against each other were Friendship Primary School, which was the school that I attended, and Lusignan Primary School. Friendship Primary was predominantly black and lusignan was predominantly east Indian.

I and two other students were picked to participate in the competition. On the day of the competition I woke up early approximately 6 a.m. Outside was still dark but the atmosphere was cool and refreshing. The swaying trees cast shadows across the wooden country. Inside the kitchen I could hear my mother hurrying about trying to prepare breakfast and get ready for work. I could hear my siblings half awoken by the sounds of pots and pans, asking what time it was. I quickly hurried to the bathroom because I knew if my sister got their before I did, I would have to wait a long time and the last thing I wanted to do was to show up late for my competition. I then got dressed in my brown uniform and beige jacket. I quickly munched on my breakfast and excused myself from the table after which I left for school. I was so excited to get to school.

Each student arrived early at school. We walked about half a mile to reach the destination where the competition was held. As we made our way up the steps, we heard loud talking in the building, but as we entered the building the room grew into total silence and all eyes gazed on us. Seats were left empty for us to sit, when we arrived. We quietly got seated. As soon as we were comfortable enough, the monitor announced the start of the competition.

During the first part of the competition something unusual happened. The monitor gave a question and before he could finish the opposite buzzed in with the right answer. At first I thought it was just an intelligent guess, but after a while the same thing occurred. I knew at that instant that something was wrong. In some of the question you had to hear the end of it before you could gave the right answer.

I began to realize what had happened. The monitor of the competition got at the competition site hours before the competition began. He was East Indian and since the school was predominantly East Indian he told them many of the answers to the questions. I thought they were scared of us winning, because prior to that competition we had won over three other primary schools. At that moment I felt really angry. I tried to buzz in even if I didn't knew the answer.

Finally the competition ended and I was anxious to hear the results. The tension was rising in the room, my heart was thumping and although my teammates were silent I could sensed that they were as nervous and anxious to hear the final results as I was.

The judges returned with the score. My heart thumped faster and I began to sweat in the palm of my hands. My foot began to shake, I began to bite my fingernails. I really felt nervous and uncomfortable. The judges announced that the school had tied. Tied? I thought to myself. We answered more questions correctly than they did. How could it be? The judges decided to give a bonus question so that one of the schools could go away with the winning trophy.

After a brief discussion amongst the judges they finally came up with the question. The question was what year did the previous president died. The room was silent, each competitor had a far away look in their eyes. They either looked up to the ceiling, down at the floor or at the judges, as if the answer would suddenly appear on these places.

I thought so hard my head began to ache. In the silence of the room I could hear the "lub-dub" of my heart as its chambers contracted and relaxed. Finally, the buzzer was sound breaking the silence and a girl from the opposite team gave an answer which was correct. Students from the school began loud cheering and talking. My heart sank. I put my head on the desk and sobbed quietly. Amongst the loud talking and laughter I heard a racial remark, one I remembered clearly was "Get out of our school you black niggers, black dunces." Our teacher quickly hurried us out the building before the situation got out of control.

On our way back no one spoke. Either they were too afraid or were angry to the extent that they couldn't speak. We walked back to our school in silence, each individual wrapped up in their own thoughts.

As I write this autobiographical piece I am dealing with the issue of racism. I'm trying to show that no matter where you go in this world you would encounter some type of prejudice, racism or indifference. One may wonder how could a little friendly high school competition involve racism.

This was the first time in my life that I had experienced racism. I knew it existed and I knew in Guyana the way blacks felt about the east Indians and vice versa. After this experience I saw the world in a different light. To me I know that everyone is created equal. However many people of different races might not believe in this theory. Some races think that they are superior to others. I understand that I cannot change the way the people in the world feels but I can understand how the world feels.

I am writing this to communicate with people who identify with this incident. As Eduardo Galeano said in his essay <u>Defense of the word</u> "One writes out of a need to communicate and commune with other, to denounce that which gives pain and to share that which gives happiness." I am writing to share with those of similar experience, to let them know that they are not alone, and help them to be brave, not afraid to speak. Galeano also said, "By revealing one's self the writer can help others to become aware of who they are."

Appendix D
Nadine's Writing Sample

TOO CLOSE FOR COMFORT

I was born on the second of August, 1977, in Kingston Jamaica, West Indies. It was a hot Tuesday, at 7:15 a.m., that I came into this world. The doctors had no problem delivering me, nor did my mother. I was given the name [Nadine Sandra Ferguson]. My mother named me [Nadine] after a model. The name [Sandra] came from England courtesy of my aunt.

Four years prior to my birth, on the twenty-fifth of September 1973, my brother [Keith] was born. It was also a Tuesday morning, but it was at 7:25 a.m. He was named after a famous British soccer player, and he later played soccer for his school. Today, he works and attends Queensborough Community College.

My mother was born in St. Thomas, the eastern part of the island of Jamaica, in a house. My father was also born in the same county. They met in high school. My mother was fifteen and my father seventeen. Both came from large families. My mother is one of sixteen children and my father is one of ten. They got married while in their early twenties, and divorced eleven years later. A combination of my mother's and father's family resulted in a very large family for me. Each of my parents' siblings has two or more children, and their children have children of their own. They are all very friendly and always welcome me to their homes. While living in Jamaica, they looked out for me because they knew that my mother was abroad.

August 28, 1982 my mother left my brother and me. At the airport in Jamaica, I was very serious and not smiling. It was one week after my birthday.

— Chu Chu, Mommy going away for two weeks. I'll bring back a lot of things for you.

I stood there speechless and serious. I had always been a serious child. In kindergarten, my teacher spanked me.

— Mommy, Miss Dunkan lick [spank] me and mi nuh trouble har.
— Teachers always hit children in order for them to learn.
— Mi nah go back a school, mi Nanny a fi teach mi a yard.

My mother left Jamaica and four years later she returned. It was November of 1986 that my life took a turn. It was a Monday, a regular school day for me. This particular day I walked home alone. I entered my yard. I began to notice that all my neighbors were staring.

— What happened?
— Nothing [Nadine].

As I stepped into my house, I noticed that there was a woman sitting at my dining table. The face was familiar but I was still puzzled. There was a picture above her. The picture was of my mother. I looked at the picture, then I looked at the woman.

— [Nadine], do you remember me?
— Yes Mommy.

Then we hugged. A month later, my brother and I were brought to the United States. I was nine and my brother thirteen.

While living in the United States I have observed the way society categorizes people. We are oppressed because of our race, culture and gender. Culture and race is not a big issue in Jamaica. Unfortunately, this is not so in the United States.

The "politics of marginalization" is a term that Dorothy Allison describes in her work, "A Question of Class." I will use this concept to show where my family fit in. The centre mainly consists of those who are middle-class whites, and the rich. On the margin are women, immigrants, the poor, and minorities. My family can be located on the margin. We are all minorities. Some of us are women and some immigrants. Most of my mother's sisters and their children are abroad. They now reside in England, Canada, and the United States.

Although there is some distance between my family and myself, I am still very close to them. However, conflicts do come about now and then. These conflicts are the result of my having adopted the American lifestyle. I dress like an American, and I talk using their slang sometimes. On my fourteenth birthday a friend of mine offered to take me to see a movie at the theatre. I accepted and thought that it would be nice to invite my cousin [Nidi] who recently migrated from Jamaica. We arrived at the theatre ten minutes before the next set of shows. Buying the tickets took forever. I like action films, but she likes the boring ones.

"I want to see an action movie," everyone agreed except [Nidi].

"I don't like violent movies, let's see Oscar." We all agreed since it was her first time, but deep down I was very upset. The movie was boring. That day I promised that I would never go to see another movie with her again.

A year later, my stepfather brought his daughter [Noreen] to live with us. I met her and exchanged words with her, but I didn't really know her. My mother has a saying, "Si me and come live with me a two different stories." You don't really know someone until you live with them. There were conflicts between us everyday.

"[Noreen], I want to buy a pair of purple jeans." Two weeks later she gets her father to buy her purple jeans. Then I buy my purple jeans. "Why did you by a purple jeans like mine, you copycat." This went on every day she spent at my house. In March 1994 she ran away after hearing she would be sent to Jamaica. It was a Tuesday morning. I got up early as usual for school.

"[Noreen], open the bathroom door." There was no answer.

"[Noreen], I am going to be late for school." There was still no answer. I went upstairs and told her father. He also tried to get her out, but there was no response. My mother and I arrived at a conclusion that she might have crawled through the bathroom window. Our rooms were in the basement so it would be a simple escape for her. Her father did not believe us until he took the screws out of the knob of the door and opened it. The bathroom was empty and the window open. [Noreen] went to school that morning, and later went to a friend's house for a week. Her father discovered this after calling her aunt in Connecticut. [Noreen] could not stay at her friends house forever. She left and went to Connecticut where she resides today. [Noreen] have not change. She now leaves her aunt's house for days, sometimes weeks. I worry about her well-being, but my life is more peaceful without her. That girl changed me. I became more violent, I began to use profanity and became very defensive. We fought day and night, over some of the most stupid things. [Noreen] always had something smart to say, and I was always prepared to defend myself.

The most recent conflict occurred during the summer of 1994. On July 23, I went to Jamaica for two weeks. Most of my time was spent at my uncle's house. All except my male cousin and his girlfriend questioned the way I dress. It was Saturday night and my cousin and I are getting clothes ready for tomorrow. A mass is being held at the Cathedral.

"[Anna] can I wear this?"

"Where is the rest of it?"

"This is all of it." The dress was an inch away from my knee. I didn't think that it looked provocative. She offered me some of her clothes but they were not my style at all. She then sent for her mother. All this was not necessary. By this time, I did not want to go anymore. Her mother sees my clothes.

"[Nadine] you nuh have notten more fi wear?"

"No."

"So wear dat den."

"Okay." During the mass, I felt very self-conscious about my attire, and did not enjoy myself. My uncle [Leonard] is a very religious person and his children are too. The Monday before my birthday, we all made plans to go to the beach. I put on my shirt and a mini-shorts with my bathing suit underneath them. I then went in my cousin's room.

"Pickni weh you clothes deh, go put on the rest of you clothes." I ignored her and went downstairs to help with the food. These are just a few of the conflicts that I had to deal with. However, this does not change the relationship between my family and myself. My mother always say, "when people are ignorant just ignore them and be intelligent."

When I think about the past, it makes me think about the future. I often wonder what it would be like, if I knew my future. My emotions change when I think about the future. Sometimes I imagine having a perfect life in the future. Other times, I think of death. Every day I say to myself, "I do not want to live in the United States forever." There are too much problems in the country. The government wants to control your life. Should abortion be legal? This should not be an issue at all. I am surrounding by drugs and drug dealers. The guilty have too many rights. If someone breaks into your home and you hurt them, you can be taken to court by that person. I also do not want to live in Jamaica again. Things have changed so much there. The prices are ridiculous. To ride the buses and vans is to risk one's life. Drivers are always racing and endangering the passengers. I could never be happy there. All the friends I had there are now abroad. Years to come, I hope to move to England or Paris and start a family of my own. But you never know what the future holds.

Appendix E
Oscar's Writing Sample

ORAL HISTORY RESEARCH—BOB MARLEY

Throughout history we have been taught about the many cultural heroes who played some vital role in bringing about social change in their society which benefited other people along with themselves. These individuals usually possesses a gift of creating public awareness which cause the persons in authority to become mindful of the fact that they are being watched and forced out of their positions if they do not answer the "voice of the people."

    A personal hero of mine and an extremely influential role model among caribbean people and the people of Jamaica is the reggae superstar and lyrical poet Robert Nesta Marley. Born in St. Ann's Parish in the year 1945, Robert Marley more affectionately called Bob Marley had to overcome poverty and suffering before he became successful through his instrumental but yet powerful messages in his music.

Bob Marley has been compared to some of the more popular known Black activists and political leaders such as Martin Luther King Jr., Marcus Garvey, Malcolm X, and Nelson Mandela. Bob Marley like these leaders was to most degree very vocal in his cry for equal rights and justice for the black and poor people of the world. The main goal in their many public speeches and in Bob Marley's case, performances, had the underlying message pleading for social change and the betterment for black people on a worldwide level.

Bob Marley spent his childhood days among uncles, aunts, and a number of other relatives. He was known as the little brown boy, this being attributed to his genetical background of mixed parentage, his mother being black and his father white. This fact however did not prevent Bob from identifying himself as black person who had to endure the harsh realities of poverty in his early life. A personal interview done with Steven Marley one of Bob's sons revealed that his father's life was much more than what the public could see. Bob Marley according to Steven was influenced greatly by his mother (Steven's Grandmother) who was a deeply religious woman that was always singing. This nurtured his father's sound sense as a youth and overall talent in music, just as how he and his brothers and sisters were nurtured by their father's many musical hits which helped to carve their present musical careers.

Bob Marley's interest in music was reflected at an early age when he took more interest in action songs than regular classwork. He was quoted in a television interview as saying "The teacher say who can write, write, and who can sing, sing. So me sing." Bob Marley was described by his teacher and mother as a bright boy but more meditative than aggressive when it came to learning. This shows the foundation which Bob Marley possessed and perfected to bring out his career as a world famous musician and speaker for the poor and Black people of the world.

Through his strong efforts and powerfully worded songs Marley was able to draw the attention of millions of people in the world including world famous leaders and presidents. He voiced a strong need for social change and equal power struggle which would benefit the many suffering black and economically stricken nations of the world. He was also particularly concerned with those nations that were being suppressed and exploited by the people in control of their governments, this included his own country of Jamaica. According to Steven Marley, his father used music to bring to light the many injustices present in the world, and the covert methods used by people in authority to manipulate the poorer and less fortunate societies of the world.

Some of Bob Marley's more famous recorded albums spoke strongly of these injustices of society or how he grew up under very poor conditions.

His deeply religious beliefs were also reflected in his songs which sometimes quoted Bible verses and how they applied to us as people in life. Bob Marley was described by Frank Owen of the New York Newsday paper as a "complex problematic figure in society." He became fabulously wealthy leaving from his career a large sum of $35 million for his children at the end of his life. He nevertheless lived a simple life observing the strict laws of his Rastafarian faith. He was also described by Owen as a gentleman who was a "reformed rudeboy" and who knew how to take care of himself in a fight.

Bob Marley was a revolutionary agitator who became a role model for Black activists everywhere, people tried to control him throughout his life especially in his early days of forming his musical career. This however only helped him to become more vocal in his cry for social change worldwide. The central struggle of his career was the navigation of a path between competing political interests which would bring about unity. The most famous of such an effort was his role played at a peace concert organized by leaders of rival political gangs in Jamaica in the late 1970's, The Jamaica Labor Party and The People's National Party. Marley was invited to perform at the concert while away from Jamaica since the previous two years on a worldwide tour. This was also the two years since a terrible shooting incident targeted at his life.

Marley had been a victim of the strong political tensions present in Jamaica in 1976 where an assassination attempt was made at his life a few minutes before he was schedule to perform at a peace concert. This incident sparked a strong concern by Marley about the politicians in Jamaica and their manipulation of the people forcing them to fight against themselves. He was able to use his unique creativity and compose songs with sweet melody which sent messages to the people of Jamaica and the world about the need for peace and the awareness of how politicians were causing them to fight each other.

Bob Marley put on an outstanding performance and an artistic selection of songs which sent a spiritual and emotional fever through the crowd of thousands of people. Marley was also able to bring to the stage front the two political leaders Mr. Edward Seaga of the Jamaica Labor Party and the Prime Minister then Mr. Michael Manley of the people's national party to shake hands. This was to show the people of Jamaica that if the leaders could have peace they could have peace. With the increasing political violence and rivalry in Jamaica at this time, no one expected that Bob Marley could have gotten his message of peace so clearly to the people.

It was seen at the point where both leaders shook hands, the bright flaring of lightning hitting the stage from the sky. Whether this was coincidental or not this made many people started to view Bob Marley not only as an entertainer but also as a prophet, the truth and cry for peace and political union in Jamaica could be heard in his songs which to present remain popular, these include "War," "Who The Cap Fit," "Guiltiness," "Redemption Songs," and "So Much Things To Say" just to name a few of his conscious songs of black and poor suppression.

Bob Marley like previous black civil rights leaders such as Martin Luther and Malcolm X had to this point of his life faced a lot of incidents where he described how people tried to either manipulate him or suppressed his career and strongly worded lyrics. There had been an assassination attempt on his life which forced him to leave Jamaica for a brief period to stay in other countries with calmer political climates. He also had several of his songs band from the air waves in Jamaica by Prime Minister Michael Manley who sought to bring the country under control in the now terrible political clashes and rivalries. Prime Minister Manley was quoted saying he would put everything under "heavy manners" which was considered inflammatory to this already critical political situation. From Literature to lyrics and T.V. or Radio programs with this stigma was censored. He was later heavily criticized by Jamaicans and opposing politicians for trying to make Jamaica into a communist country. Bob Marley himself became even more critical of the situation and now wrote more songs and gave more performances criticizing politicians and their abuse of power.

In the final analysis of his life Bob Marley had been successful in spreading his message to the world. He took control of his divided country and by the period leading up to the end of his life he made many Jamaicans and people worldwide realize that there was more to life than just money and power. He became very famous for his humble way of life despite being in an elite class and managed to gain worldwide respect for his words of wisdom. A particularly strong note from his son Steven Marley when asked about his father's simple outlook on life was that his father lived for people and not for himself this was the only thing that made him happy in life and so he reaped the benefits of this approach.

My personal view of Bob Marley's efforts is that without his presence and worldwide cry for peace many of the changes which took place eventually would not have happened. As a result I think we as black people should be thankful for all of these black activists who spent a great portion of their lives fighting for our advancement. The talent of these individuals was used unselfishly to help us enjoy most of what we are able to enjoy today and with this in mind I don't think any praise is too great for their work and others who history may not have mentioned or focussed on but also paid dearly for whatever sacrifices they made.

Notes

1. The names of all students have been changed to protect their anonymity.
2. By "anglophone Caribbean," I am referring to all of the following islands: Anguilla, Antigua and Barbuda, the Bahamas, Barbados, the British Virgin Islands, Caricou, Dominica, Grenada, the Grenadines, Jamaica, Montserrat, Nevis, St. Kitts, St. Lucia, St. Vincent, Trinidad and Tobago, as well as Belize in Central America and Guyana on the mainland of South America. Guyana and Belize have been included because of their shared history of British colonization with the other Caribbean islands. The region is also commonly referred to as the "West Indies." For the purposes of this study, the focus will be on immigrant students from Guyana and Jamaica.
3. Since this study was conducted, a number of structural changes have occurred in the writing program at LIU: English 13 and 14 are now worth three credits each even though classes still meet for six contact hours a week, all workshops have been eliminated, and the English 14 exit examination has been reinstated.

4. The term "East Indian" is used to refer to Guyanese whose ancestors were brought to Guyana from India to work as indentured laborers on the sugar plantations to alleviate the labor shortage created by the abolition of slavery in the West Indies in 1838. Indentureship was discontinued about 1917.

References

Alleyne, M. (1980). *Comparative Afro-American.* Ann Arbor: Karoma Publishers.

_____. (1987, January-March). Creole language and the Caribbean community. *Caricom Perspective,* 24-26.

_____. (1994). Problems of standardization of creole languages. In M. Morgan (Ed.), *The social construction of identity in creole situations* (pp. 7-18). Los Angeles: Center for Afro-American Studies, UCLA.

Allsopp, R. (1979). Caribbean English and our schools. *Caribbean Journal of Education,* 6(2), 99-110.

_____. (1996). *Dictionary of Caribbean English usage.* New York: Oxford University Press.

Anderson, W., & Grant, R. (1987). *The new newcomers.* Toronto: Canadian Scholars Press.

Ball, A. (1992). Cultural preference and the expository writing of African-American adolescents. *Written Communication,* 9(4), 501-532.

Ballard, B. & Clanchy, J. (1991). Assessment by misconception: Cultural influences and intellectual traditions. In L. Hamp-Lyons (Ed.), *Assessing second language writing in academic contexts* (pp. 19-36). Norwood, NJ: Ablex.

Bereiter, C. & Engelmann, S. (1966). *Teaching disadvantaged children in the preschool.* Englewood Cliff, NJ: Prentice-Hall.

Bickerton, D. (1981). *Roots of language.* Ann Arbor: Karoma Publishers.
Bizzell, P. (1984, March). *What happens when basic writers come to college?* Paper presented at the annual meeting of the Conference on College Composition and Communication, New York, NY.
Bonnett, A. (1981). *Institutional adaptation of West Indian immigrants to America.* Washington, DC: University Press of America.
Carrington, L. (1992, November 28). In D. Sontag. Caribbean pupils' English seems barrier, not bridge. *The New York Times,* pp. A1, A22.
Chafe, W. & Danielewicz, J. (1987). Properties of spoken and written language. In R. Horowitz & S. J. Samuels (Eds.), *Comprehending oral and written language* (pp. 83-113). San Diego, CA: Academic Press.
Cheshire, J. (1991). Introduction: Sociolinguistics and English around the world. In J. Cheshire (Ed.), *English around the world* (pp. 1-12). Cambridge: Cambridge University Press.
Christie. P. (1983). Language and social change in Jamaica. *Journal of Caribbean Studies, 3*(3), 204-228.
Coelho, E. (1991). *Caribbean students in Canadian schools. Book II.* Ontario: Pippin Publishing Limited.
Coleman, C. (1995). *Negotiating literacies: Profiles of two African-American college students.* Unpublished doctoral dissertation, Teachers College, Columbia University, New York, NY.
Craig, D. (1971). Education and Creole English in the West Indies. In D. Hymes (Ed.), *Pidginization and creolization of languages* (pp. 371-391). Cambridge: Cambridge University Press.
Cummins, J. (1984). *Bilingualism and special education: Issues in assessment and pedagogy.* Austin, TX: Pro-ed.
Dalphinis, M. (1985). *Caribbean and African languages: Social history, language, literature and education.* London: Karia Press.
DeCamp, D. (1971). Introduction: The study of pidgin and creole languages. In D. Hymes (Ed.), *Pidginization and creolization of languages* (pp. 13-39). Cambridge: Cambridge University Press.
Devonish, H. (1986). *Language and liberation: Creole language politics in the Caribbean.* London: Karia Press.
Dillard, J. L. (1972). *Black English.* New York: Random House.
Dugger, C. (1997, January 12). For half a million, this is still the new world. *The New York Times,* p. 27.
Edwards, V. (1983). *Language in multicultural classrooms.* London: Batsford Academic and Educational Ltd.
Edwards, V. & Redfern, A. (1992). *The world in a classroom: Language education in Britain and Canada.* Avon, England: Multilingual Matters Ltd.
Farr, M. (1993). Essayist literacy and other verbal performances. *Written Communication, 10*(1), 4-38.
Foner, N. (1987). Introduction: New immigrants and changing patterns in New York City. In N. Foner (Ed.), *New immigrants in New York* (pp. 1-33). New York: Columbia University Press.
Gee, J. (1990). *Social linguistics and literacies: Ideology and discourses.* London: The Falmer Press.

Giles, H., Coupland, J., & Coupland, N. (Eds.). (1991). *Contexts of accommodation: Developments in applied sociolinguistics.* Cambridge: Cambridge University Press.
Gilyard, K. (1991). *Voices of the self: A study of language competence.* Detroit, MI: Wayne State University Press.
Gopaul-McNicol, S. (1993). *Working with West Indian families.* New York: Guilford Press.
Halliday, M. A. K. (1989). *Spoken and written language.* Oxford: Oxford University Press.
Halliday, M. A. K. & Hasan, R. (1976). *Cohesion in English.* New York: Longman Group Limited.
Holm. J. (1985, April). *The Creole core: Grammatical interference in college composition.* Paper presented at the annual meeting of Teachers of English to Speakers of Other Languages, New York, NY.
_____. (1988). *Pidgins and creoles: Volume I.* Cambridge: Cambridge University Press.
Hymes, D. (1980). Commentary. In A. Valdman & A. Highfield (Eds.), *Theoretical orientations in creole studies* (pp. 389-423). New York: Academic Press.
Irish, J. A. G. (1997, February 24-March 9). Towards a new policy for educating creole-speaking students. *The Caribbean American,* p. 5.
Kasinitz, P. (1992). *Caribbean New York: Black immigrants and the politics of race.* New York: Cornell University Press.
Labov, W. (1981). *The study of nonstandard English.* Urbana, IL: National Council of Teachers of English.
LePage, R. & Tabouret-Keller, A. (1985). *Acts of identity: Creole-based approaches to language and ethnicity.* Cambridge: Cambridge University Press.
LIU. (1995) *Handbook for English composition teachers.* Brooklyn, NY: Long Island University.
London, C. (1980). *Teaching and learning with Caribbean students.* New York, NY: Teachers College, Columbia University. (ERIC Document Reproduction Service No. ED 196 977).
McGroarty, M. (1996). Language attitudes, motivation and standards. In S. L.McKay & N. Hornberger (Eds.), *Sociolinguistics and language teaching* (pp. 3-46). Cambridge: Cambridge University Press.
McKay, S. L. (1996). Literacy and literacies. In S. L. McKay & N. Hornberger (Eds.), *Sociolinguistics and language teaching* (pp. 421-445). Cambridge: Cambridge University Press.
McKay, S. L. & Wong, S. C. (1988). Preface. In S. L. McKay & S. C. Wong (Eds.), *Language diversity: Problem or resource?* (pp. vii-x). Boston: Heinle and Heinle Publishers.
Morgan, M. (1994). Introduction: In M. Morgan (Ed.), *Language and the social construction of identity in creole situations* (pp. 1-6). Los Angeles: Center for Afro-American Studies Publications, UCLA.
Narvaez, D. & Garcia, M. (1992). *Meeting the needs of newly-arrived West Indian students in New York public schools.* New York: Teachers College, Columbia University. (ERIC Document Reproduction Service No. ED 359 307).
Nichols, P. (1996). Pidgins and creoles. In S. L. McKay & N. Hornberger (Eds.), *Sociolinguistics and language teaching* (pp. 195-217). Cambridge: Cambridge University Press.
Olson, D. (1977a). From utterance to text: The bias of language in speech and writing. *Harvard Educational Review, 47,* 257-281.

_____. (1977b). The languages of instruction: The literate bias of schooling. In R. Anderson, R. Spiro & W. E. Montague (Eds.), *Schooling and the acquisition of knowledge* (pp. 65-89). Hillsdale, NJ: Lawrence Erlbaum Associates.

Ong, W. (1977). *Interfaces of the word.* Ithaca, NY: Cornell University Press.

_____. (1982). *Orality and literacy: The technologizing of the word.* New York: Routledge.

Palmer, R. (1995). *Pilgrims from the sun: West Indian migration to America.* New York: Twayne Publishers.

Pratt, M. L. (1995). Arts of the contact zone. In D. Bartholomae & A. Petrosky (Eds.), *Reading the lives of others* (pp. 179-198). Boston: Bedford Books.

Pratt-Johnson, Y. (1993). Curriculum for Jamaican Creole-speaking students in New York City. *World Englishes, 12*(2), 257-264.

Rickford, J. (1987). *Dimensions of a creole continuum.* Stanford: Stanford University Press.

_____. (1996). Regional and social variation. In S. L. McKay & N. Hornberger (Eds.), *Sociolinguistics and language teaching* (pp. 151-194). Cambridge: Cambridge University Press.

_____. (1999). *African American Vernacular English.* Malden, MA: Blackwell Publishers.

Rivera-Batiz, F. (1994). The multicultural population of New York City: A socioeconomic profile of the mosaic. In F. Rivera-Batiz (Ed.), *Reinventing urban education* (pp. 23-68). New York: Institute for Urban and Minority Education (IUME) Press, Teachers College, Columbia University.

Roberts, P. (1988). *West Indians and their language.* Cambridge: Cambridge University Press.

Ruiz, R. (1988). Orientations in language planning. In S. L. McKay & S. C. Wong (Eds.), *Language diversity: Problem or resource?* (pp. 3-26). Boston: Heinle and Heinle Publishers.

Schieffelin, B. & Cochran-Smith, M. (1984). Learning to read culturally: Literacy before schooling. In H. Goelman, A. Oberg & F. Smith (Eds.), *Awakening to literacy* (pp. 3-23). Portsmouth, NH: Heinemann Educational Books.

Scollon, R., & Scollon, S. B. (1981). *Narrative, literacy and face in interethnic communication.* Norwood, NJ: Ablex.

Selinker, L. (1983). Interlanguage. In B. Robinett & J. Schacter (Eds.), *Second language learning: Contrastive analysis, error analysis and related aspects* (pp. 173-196). Ann Arbor: The University of Michigan Press.

Shaughnessy, M. (1977). *Errors and expectations: A guide for teachers of basic writing.* New York: Oxford University Press.

Smitherman, G. (1994, November). *From the hood to the amen corner.* Keynote address delivered at the Conference on Language and Power: African American Perspectives, Teachers' College, Columbia University, New York, NY.

Solomon, R. P. (1992). *Black resistance in high school: Forging a separatist culture.* New York: State University of New York Press.

Sontag, D. (1992, November 28). Caribbean pupils' English seems barrier, not bridge. *The New York Times,* pp. A1, A22.

Street, B. (1991). *Cross-cultural literacy.* Paper presented at the Conference on Intergenerational Literacy. Teachers College, Columbia University, New York, NY.

Thompson, M. (1984). Teaching literacy to Creole speakers: Problems and possibilities. *Caribbean Journal of Education, 11*(2-3), 158-183.

Walters, K. (1994). Writing and education. In H. Gunther & O. Ludwig (Eds.), *Schrift und Schriftlichkeit/Writing and its use* (pp. 638-645). Berlin: Walter de Gruyter.

Winer, L. (1993). Teaching speakers of Caribbean English Creoles in North American classrooms. In A. W. Glowka & D. Lance (Eds.), *Language variation in North American English* (pp. 191-198). New York: MLA.

Winford, D. (1991). The Caribbean. In J. Cheshire (Ed.), *English around the world* (pp. 565-584). Cambridge: Cambridge University Press.

_____. (1994). Sociolinguistic approaches to language use in the anglophone Caribbean. In M. Morgan (Ed.), *Language and the social construction of identity in creole situations* (pp. 43-62). Los Angeles: Center for Afro-American Studies Publications, UCLA.

Author Index

A
Alleyne, M., 11, 12, 32, 128, 129, *161*
Allsopp, R., 3, 26, 69, 106, *161*
Anderson, W., 2, 16, *161*

B
Ball, A., 2, *161*
Ballard, B., 24, *161*
Bereiter, C., 132, *161*
Bickerton, D., 5, 129, *162*
Bizzell, P., 23, *162*
Bonnett, A., 9, 17, *162*

C
Carrington, L., 5, *162*
Chafe, W., 22, 37, 48, 50, 111, *162*
Cheshire, J., 3, 137, *162*
Christie, P., 7, *162*
Clanchy, J., 24, *161*
Cochran-Smith, M., 20, *164*
Coelho, E., 2, 16, 58, *162*
Coleman, C., 2, 53, *162*
Coupland, J., 118, *163*
Coupland, N., 118, *163*
Craig, D., 18, *162*
Cummins, J., 21, *162*

D
Dalphinis, M., 12, *162*
Danielewicz, J., 22, 37, 48, 50, 71, 111, *162*
DeCamp, D., 6, *162*
Devonish, H., 7, *162*
Dillard, J. L., 18, *162*
Dugger, C., 9, *162*

E

Edwards, V., 15, 16, *162*
Engelmann, S., 132, *161*

F

Farr, M., 21, 23, 120, 126, 132, *162*
Foner, N., 8, *162*

G

Garcia, M., 2, 13, 14, *163*
Gee, J., 24, 80, *162*
Giles, J., 118, *163*
Gilyard, K., 132, *163*
Gopaul, -McNicol, S., 17, *163*
Grant, R., 2, 16, *161*

H

Halliday, M. A. K., 22, 37, 46, 48, 65, 69, 85, 105, *163*
Hasan, R., 69, 85, 105, *163*
Holm, J., 2, 26, 129, *163*
Hymes, D., 137, *163*

I

Irish, J. A. G., 19, *163*

K

Kasinitz, P., 8, *163*

L

Labov, W., 133, *163*
LePage, R., 3, 7, 118, *163*
LIU, 30, *163*
London, C., 19, *163*

M

McGroarty, M., 128, 131, *163*
McKay, S. L., 20, 134, *163*
Morgan, M., 8, 131, *163*

N

Narvaez, D., 2, 13, 14, *163*
Nichols, P., 128, *163*

O

Olson, D., 21, 63, *163*
Ong, W., 21, 48, 50, *164*

P

Palmer, R., 8, *164*
Pratt, M. L., 27, *164*
Pratt-Johnson, Y., 2, 18, *164*

R

Redfern, A., 15, 16, *162*
Rickford, J., 6, 32, 35, 41, 62, 128, 131, 133, *164*
Rivera-Batiz, F., 9, *164*
Roberts, P., 6, 25, 39, 57, *164*
Ruiz, R., 20, *164*

S

Schieffelin, B., 20, *164*
Scollon, R., 4, 21, *164*
Scollon, S. B., 4, 21, *164*
Selinker, L., 25, *164*
Shaughnessy, M., 2, 53, 68, 125, *164*
Smitherman, G., 131, *164*
Solomon, R. P., 2, 16, 17, *164*
Sontag, D., 18, 19, *164*
Street, B., 21, 22, *164*

T

Tabouret-Keller, A., 3, 7, 118, *163*
Thompson, M., 13, *164*

W

Walters, K., 21, 23, *165*
Winer, L., 2, 8, 19, 26, *165*
Winford, D., 6, 8, 11, 12, 32, 62, *165*
Wong, S. C., 134, *163*

Subject Index

A

academic interlanguage, 25-26, 64, 69, 120
academic writing, 24, 108, 120
acrolect, 6, 7, 32, 128
African American Vernacular English (AAVE), 2, 4, 18, 23, 130-131, 135
assimilationist, 15-16, 132-133

B

basic writers, 2, 23
basic writing program, LIU, 29-31, 115, 159
basilect, 6, 14, 32
Black English, 18
broken English, 6, 82, 127

C

Caribbean Academic Program (CAP), 18
Caribbean Examinations Council (CXC), 103
Caribbean students in
  Canada, 16-17
  England, 14-15
  United States, 13-14, 17-20
colonization, British, 6-8, 128-130, 159
Common Entrance Examination, 42, 101
compensatory education, 15, 132
copula, zero, 26, 39, 54, 124
correctness, syntactic, 107, 119-120
cover letter, portfolio, 34, 70-1, 90-91, 108, 121-122

170 SUBJECT INDEX

creole continuum, 6, 11, 25
Creolese, 42, 127

D

discourse, 24-25, 80
discourse analysis, 46, 64, 84, 104
discourse features, 27, 119

E

East Indian, 6, 65-66, 146-147, 160
eradicationist, 132-133
errors, 54-55, 75, 116, 125
ESL, 12-14, 16, 18, 29-30, 51
essayist literacy, 4, 21, 23
essayist writing, 4, 22, 67-69, 87, 89
essays, 30-31, 34, 67-69, 84-90, 104-108, 120-122, 127
exit exam, 50, 159

F

formal writing, 30, 64, 84, 104, 120-122
front focusing, 26, 56, 124

G

Guyanese Creole English, 1, 32, 35, 56

I

identity, linguistic, 4, 7
immigration, Caribbean, 7-10, 51-52
in-class writing, 30-31, 50, 71-72, 90, 109-110, 121
inflection, zero, 25-26, 39-40, 54, 56, 75-77, 95-96, 112-113, 124
informal writing, 30, 46, 91, 119-120
interlanguage, 13, 25, 123
interviews, 32-36

J

Jamaican Creole English, 32, 35, 82

L

language attitudes, 2, 3, 4, 7-8, 127-130
language planning, 131-134
language policy, 4, 135
language vs. dialect, 4, 11-15
lexical density, 22, 38-39, 52-53, 68, 74-75, 94, 111, 122-123
literacy, models of, 20
Long Island University (LIU), 9, 29-30, 45

M

Marley, Bob, 110-111, 155-158
mesolect, 6, 32
morphosyntactic features, 27, 53-54, 75, 95, 112, 124

N

native speaker, 3, 14, 16, 137
nonnative speaker, 3, 19, 137
nonstandard English, 130-133, 137

O

oral history, 31, 72-74
oral language, 21-25, 48, 50, 69
overgeneralization, 39-40, 78, 97, 113-114, 124

P

patois, 62, 82, 127
pedagogy, language, 12-14
pidgin, 5, 18, 129
placement test, 23, 30, 64, 84, 103, 125-126, 139-140
plagiarism, 52-53, 74-75, 80
plurals, 26, 40, 56, 77-78, 95-96, 113
portfolios, writing, 31, 34
possessives, 26, 56
pronunciation, 34-35, 62, 83

R

research papers, 31, 39, 50-53, 72-75, 79-80, 92-95, 110-112, 122

S

sentence focus, 26, 40
spelling, 35, 56-57, 78-79, 124
staggered migration, 43, 63
standard English, 3, 7, 12-14, 16, 25-26, 39-40, 102, 118-119, 128-133, 136-137
Standard English as a Second Dialect (SESD), 16-17
style shifting, 7, 117-118
subject/verb agreement, 26, 76, 96

T

teacher preparation, 135-136
transfer, language, 39
type/token ratio, 22, 38-39, 52-53, 75, 94, 122-123

V

verb participles, 26, 40, 77
vernacular, 5, 7, 97, 127-128

W

western linguistic tradition, 98, 129-131
West Indies, 159-160
workshops, writing, 30-31
written language, 21-25, 37-39, 69

OHIO UNIVERSITY LIBRARY

Please return this book as soon as you have finished with it. In order to avoid a fine it must be returned by the latest date stamped below. All books are subject to recall after two weeks or immediately if needed for reserve.

CF